ITALIAN
MOTOR CYCLES

GUIDE TO
ITALIAN
MOTOR CYCLES
C J AYTON

TEMPLE PRESS

© Copyright Charles Herridge Ltd 1985

First published 1985 by
Temple Press
an imprint of Newnes Books
84-88 The Centre
Feltham, Middlesex TW13 4BH
a division of
The Hamlyn Publishing Group Limited
and distributed for them by
The Hamlyn Publishing Group Limited
Rushden, Northants, England

Produced by Charles Herridge Limited
Woodacott, Northam, Bideford, Devon EX39 1NB

ISBN 0 600 35141 6

Printed in England

Foreword

Now and for the past 15 years motor cycle enthusiasts with an eye for a machine conceived a continent or two west of Hamamatsu have had no choice other than to buy Italian. Not, in the majority of cases, that doing so has been a hardship. The police forces of Europe and some of its middle-aged citizens may have been seduced by the apparently unchanging line, and long-term worth, of the German BMW. More carefree motor cyclists, on the other hand, with less money to blow but fewer hangups about how they do so, have never been able to resist the sheer style, and performance, of Italian machines.

Criticisms of the poor paint and plating and dodgy ancillaries found on these vulpine thoroughbreds fall on un-regarding ears. Riders of Italian bikes simply *know* they are the best in the world. Paintwork and similar ephemera are of little concern to them: what matters is the solid worth of race-proved engines built by hand and shoe-horned into frames designed and tested by hard-riding men who wouldn't know a computer terminal from Grand Central Station.

And when talk turns to how the bikes look, Italophiles are on even safer ground. The most habitual fence-percher must acknowledge the racy lines, the urgency, that distinguish the best – which are usually also the fastest – of the Italian bikes and linger, as a residual grace, in less exalted examples of the breed.

It is also true, of course, that until quite recently many of them exhibited less endearing traits – such as weather-sensitive starting – that have been cited by riders of more mundane motor cycles as good and sufficient reason for abstaining from Italian-bike ownership.

That Italy's motor cycles are in the enviable position of being the only real alternative world-wide to the Japanese owes much to the uncompromising ways of the industrialist Alessandro de Tomaso. When he assumed a commanding position in the late 1960s, after acquiring Moto Guzzi and Benelli, de Tomaso played so skilfully on the nationalism, and the commercial instincts, of government and big business that tariff restrictions were imposed, reducing the threatened flood of Japanese imports to a trickle. In these protected circumstances de Tomaso – in company, possible to his chagrin, with rivals at home – built a vigorous industry. Thwarted in Italy, the Japanese had little option but to concentrate their energies, in their European strategies, on the hapless British who, lacking a de Tomaso, quickly succumbed to the onslaught from the East.

But Japanese hype has never weakened the loyalty to country, and usually brand, that is felt by motor cyclists addicted to Italian machines. There may be some consumer movement between Moto this and Moto that; but it is not widespread. Only, finally, a distaste for chain-adjusting makes otherwise contented *Ducatisti* switch to one of Signor de Tomaso's products. To explain a reverse trend, Ducati riders point to the revvability of the desmo engine and rest their case.

This book, more than others in the series, purports to be no more than a partial selection, for review, made from many machines currently and previously on offer. The very latest have not been commented on; nor the earliest.

The compiler offers thanks for the invaluable help, with "background" and photographs, of Alan Wraight and for material provided by, among others, D. L. Minton, Val Ward, C. E. Allen, M. R. Wigan and Bruce Preston. For boning-up on race references, no finer source was possible, or sought, than Vic Willoughby's published writings.

Aermacchi

Aermacchi bear the distinction of having produced the best-developed ohv road-racing single of all time: a prodigious achievement for a company that spent almost forty years making aeroplanes before turning, in 1951–52, to the manufacture of two-wheelers. The first Aermacchi to be marketed was as much scooter as motor cycle, having semi-enclosure for most working parts, footboards, and an under-saddle engine; the fuel tank, however, was in a conventional "motor cycle" position and the wheels were of reasonably large diameter, at 17in. In 1953 the first model, known as the Convertible, was succeeded by the Zeffiro, an improved version with either 125 or 150cc light-alloy two-stroke engine and catalogued as being capable of 45–55mph. These later models had telescopic front forks in place of the Convertible's spindly-looking leading-link layout but retained much of the original scooter appearance through their deeply valanced mud-guards and generous front panelling.

The first true all-motor cycle Aermacchi was the 125cc Monsone of 1955, which was followed by the 150 Corsaro. Both had pivoted-fork rear suspension, with enclosure for the final chain, and telescopic forks; the engines were marginally developed versions of the first two-strokes and were harnessed to a four-speed gearbox.

It was the then futuristic-looking Chimera of 1956 that had the first ohv four-stroke engine to be made at Aermacchi. It was fitted in the horizontal position that was to become the hallmark of Aermacchi design. The layout was chosen by Ing. Alfredo Bianchi to give a low centre of gravity, for the best possible handling. The pushrod engine had horizontal finning and a bore and stroke of 60 x 61mm (for a 175cc version) and 66 x 72mm (250cc), with a compression ratio, in both cases, of 7:1. Top speeds were claimed to be 66 and 72mph; both models had a four-speed gearbox.

As noteworthy as the engine was the Chimera's body, designed by Mario Ravelli. It enclosed most of the engine, rear drive and wheel and, surprisingly, contrived to look rather elegant. The front forks were of telescopic type and

Aermacchi's 1970 Ala Verda 250 with 66 × 72mm, 18bhp engine and five-speed gearbox weighed 270lb and had a top speed of almost 90mph.

carried a fixed, deep-valanced mudguard. The brakes were of 8in diameter, in full-width alloy hubs. "Sleek and gentlemanly", one observer has called the Chimera. It was successful, too, for it remained in production until 1960.

In 1957 Aermacchi acted on a belated discovery that Italians were (and are) addicted to fast motor cycles. This was the year of their first sporting models, included in a range of four identified as Ala Bianca, Ala Azzurra, Ala Rossa and Ala Verda. The Bianca and Azzurra were "turismo" models powered by 175cc (60 x 61mm) and 250cc (66 x 72mm) ohv singles operating on a 7:1 compression ratio. The frame was new on all, of spine type, the engine/gear unit depending from it, with the barrel a few degrees up from the horizontal. The 175 Rossa and 250 Verda were the sports models. These had higher-compression engines than the other two, and dropped bars, with a short, racy-looking dualseat and an 8in-diameter double brake in the front wheel. Power output of the Verda, the most popular of the quartet, was 18bhp at 6,800rpm, and top speed nearly 80mph.

Aermacchi's scooter obsession was not easily allowed to die. In 1957–58 they produced the Biccindrico, named thus because it represented a break with brief tradition in having an ohv twin engine. (For the rest, it followed the familiar theme of partial enclosure.) There were two further scooters, after the twin, which did not sell in any number; and then, apparently, Aermacchi realised they had left it too late to climb on the Vespa/Lambretta bandwagon. Thereafter they concentrated on motor cycles, usually with a sporting flavour.

The Ala d'Oro (Golden Wing) models, produced from 1958 to 1961 in 175 and 250 capacities, had high-dome pistons (giving 9:1 and 9.5:1 cr), race cams, extra-strength valve springs and polished ports. The 175 ran on a straight-through exhaust system, the 250 had a shallow-taper megaphone. The 18in wheels had alloy rims and racing tyres (2.50in front, 2.75in rear), and special fittings included a tachometer and rear-set footrests. Both models enjoyed a fair success in Italian production racing and were credited with top speeds of 93–94mph and 102mph.

A minor foray into the cross-country world, with the 250 Cross single, was less successful. Competition from lighter, and probably more powerful, models imported from Husqvarna, Greeves and Jawa/CZ was too much for the Cross.

In 1960 Aermacchi passed into the control of the American company of Harley-Davidson. It was not unexpected. Aermacchi had found it difficult to survive at home, in a land dominated by the scooter giants and the old-established motor cycle firms of Moto Guzzi and Gilera. Exports were derisory. There had been exploratory talks with the Americans in 1959. Harley-Davidson, locked into their image of big vee-twins of around one litre, were concerned about missing sales in the buoyant US market to the newcomers who wanted to buy motor cycles similar to the 250–500 twins popularised by the Japanese.

The Italian connection seemed an inspired solution to the H-D management. The Italian end was renamed Aermacchi-Harley-Davidson and the first-born of the union was christened Wisconsin. It was an Ala Verda, suitably modified, mainly by substitution of high-rise handlebars for the original dropped pattern.

Later in the 60s this 250 became the Sprint, with a five-speed gearbox. The 66 x 72mm engine ran on a compression ratio of 8.5:1 and produced 18bhp at 6,750rpm for a top speed of almost 85mph. In 1968 it was joined by a 350 known as the GTS in Italy and as the Sprint 350 in other parts of Europe and in the USA. With traditional, horizontal layout, the 350's engine had 74 x 80mm measurements and power output was claimed to be 25bhp at 7,000rpm, which was not exceptionally high but enough, in view of the under-300lb weight of the machine, to provide near-500 performance.

Strangely, perhaps, it was American influence that directed Aermacchi into road-racing. The first racing 250 Ala d'Oro was intended for production-class

The Aermacchi 350, as designed for the US market, featured a finned enclosure for the valve chest, to mate with the cylinder head, a carburettor with integral float chamber, and twin silencers (not evident in this view).

competition; it was even sold complete with lighting equipment. In 1961 it was sharpened up. The compression ratio was raised to 10.2:1 and the carburettor became a 30mm Dellorto; power rose to 30bhp at 9,600rpm and maximum speed, with the bike in faired form, to 125mph. Weight was 230lb and handling, as ever, impressively good. This was the DS model and it was made up to 1964, when the four-speed gearbox was exchanged for a five-speed and bore/stroke dimensions were altered to an oversquare ratio, at 72 x 61mm, for a revs ceiling of 10,200 and a maximum speed of 130mph. In 1963 the 250 had been joined by a racing 350 Ala d'Oro, more usually known as the DS350, having a 74 x 80mm unit producing 33bhp at 7,800rpm, for 127mph. Race results were variously rewarding and disappointing. There were plenty of breakdowns, usually through troubles with connecting rods and valves; however, international placings included sixths in the Belgian and Ulster grands prix and a succession of fourths in Czechoslovakia, Holland and Germany. In 1966, after the 350 had received some frame-stiffening attention

Norman – brother of John – Surtees at speed on his Aermacchi at Brands Hatch in 1963.

and an extra gear ratio, Renzo Pasolini rose to third in the final table for the 350cc world championship. A production version of this improved model, running on an 11:1 compression ratio and turning out 38bhp at 8,500rpm, was made available in 1967.

First-born of the Aermacchi-Harley-Davidson union in 1960: the 250 Wisconsin, based on the Ala Verda.

The factory team of 1968 was equipped with very special 350s. By then the management considered the 250cc class a lost cause – a prey to the high-revving Japanese two-strokes. The 77 x 75mm 350s were fitted with an outside flywheel and a 38mm carburettor and were said to give 42bhp at the rear wheel, and 50 (SAE) at the crankshaft. All-up weight, with full fairing, was 250lb. Kelvin Carruthers, the leading rider, was always a threat to Agostini, on the MV Agusta three, and finished the season in third position in the championship. The following year, in the Isle of Man, Carruthers was timed at 131.4mph, only 1.4mph down on the fastest Yamaha.

Another interesting project at Aermacchi was a Lino Tonti-designed 500cc Linto twin, which was built in 1967–68 and raced intermittently in 1968 and 1969. Tonti had used two 250 cylinders on a specially cast crankcase and power output was good ... in excess of 60bhp, it was said. Alberto Pagani rode a Linto to second place in the 1968 Dutch GP and won the GP of the Nations at Imola the following year.

While the 350 single was still, at the end of the 60s, a near-match for other Italian four-strokes, no matter whether multi-cylindered and dohc, complete takeover of the class by the Japanese two-strokes was seen to be only a matter of time. Aermacchi turned to the two-stroke. The race shop began working on 250 and 350cc watercooled twins that were to bring four world championships to Varese.

In 1972 Pasolini rode Aermacchi two-strokes to second and third respectively in the 250 and 350cc championships. Then, in 1973, he was killed in a multiple crash at Monza which also claimed the life of Jarno Saarinen, the brilliant Swedish rider who had forced his Yamaha ahead of Pasolini in the struggle for the 1972 250 championship. In 1974 and '75 the 250 Aermacchi, by then identified as a Harley-Davidson, and ridden by Walter Villa, won the championship. In 1976 he made it a hat-trick, and then capped that with a win in the 350cc class. The Japanese were forced to acknowledge that two-stroke know-how existed in Europe.

The 250 two-stroke had a bore and stroke of 56 x 50mm and gave 56bhp at the rear wheel, while the 64 x 54mm 350 was good for 68bhp. A six-speed gearbox was specified in both cases.

Despite these results, Harley-Davidson were losing interest in their Italian offshoot. Sales of the Italian-styled

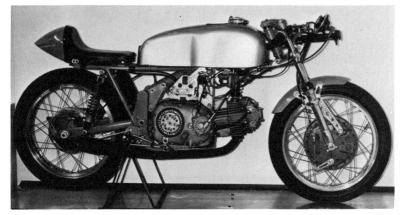

Francis Beart prepared this 1968 350 Aermacchi which went on to win the 1970 Junior Manx Grand Prix.

Aermacchi racer of 1967 (photographed in 1983) sporting a Rickman frame built to guidelines suggested by Othmar Drixl.

lightweights in the USA had never reached the hoped-for heights. H-D were feeling the pinch financially and there appeared to be sound reasoning in a sellout; which is what happened, in 1978, to the Italian firm of Cagiva.

Aermacchi Drixton

The Drixton was based on a "Rickmanised" Aermacchi, itself the product of Swiss–Italian engineer

Othmar Drixl's determination to provide improved running gear for the 350 production-racer Aermacchi. This lightweight four-stroke, with its generous ground clearance, had proved more than a match for Manx Nortons and 7R AJSs in the early 1960s. However, its normally adequate handling could be faulted on the bumps and swerves of a natural road course such as the TT circuit in the Isle of Man. Drixl approached the Rickman brothers in

England and the result was a superior frame for the Aermacchi, based on proven Metisse lines, that elicited much praise from the few riders who managed to buy, and race, an example.

Drixl remained unsatisfied. In 1967–68 he contacted Egidio Baroni of Milan, a frame builder and motor cycle engineer of high repute. Between them the two evolved a third version of the Aermacchi racer. This was the Drixton, which became available in kit form (less engine) in the UK for £350.

The Drixton followed the Metisse in abandoning the standard spine-type frame in favour of a multi-tube layout, in which the engine was suspended from the horizontal section of a pair of tubes sweeping first downward from the steering head and then to the rear, to join the triangulated rear frame. The base of the engine-gear unit – located almost horizontally, in standard Aermacchi fashion – was secured by extensions of the rear frame. There was a further pair of tubes running between steering head and the mount for the rear-fork suspension units; apart from this basic role, they also supported the glass-fibre fuel tank and the seat. Complete, triangulated support of the steering head was achieved by an additional member running from the top back to a midway point on the upper rails.

Metisse-like refinements included eccentric adjusters for the rear-wheel spindle. Baroni front forks and rear-suspension units were styled on Ceriani lines. The large brakes, in full-width hubs, were by Fontana.

Lower and narrower than a standard Aermacchi, the Drixton was welcomed by riding talent of the calibre of Kelvin Carruthers and Ray Pickrell who found its handling most impressive.

Specification

Drixton (1968) *Single-cylinder, ohv, four-stroke. 344cc (74 x 80mm). Four-speed. 4.5g fuel. Tyres, 3.25 x 18in (fr), 3.50 x 18in (r). 130mph.*

Benelli

Benelli was founded by six Benelli brothers in 1911; perhaps five would be a more sensible calculation, for the youngest of the six, Tonino, was only six at the time. It was Tonino who took the firm into racing in 1923 when, aged 18, he entered for a meeting at Monza, on a

Ted Mellors' 1939 Lightweight TT-winning Benelli. Fitted to the front of the one-gallon oil tank is a cooler, in this photograph seen with a cover over the honeycomb for rapid warm-up during training. Rear suspension is by pivoting fork linked to springs carried in the vertical containers and damped by friction units.

specially prepared 150, and took fourth place.

Developed into a 175, with a twin-cam head, this machine carried Tonino to Italian championship titles in the late 1920s and formed the basis for the dohc 250 used by Ted Mellors for his famous IoM TT victory of 1939. A 500 developed by the factory in 1935 was less successful and was withdrawn after dismal outings at Tripoli and Monza. The 250, however, flourished from its inception. With external flywheel, dohc, hairpin valve springs and a rev-range extending almost to 9,000, it was good for 110mph and had the legs of many 350s. Total weight, less fuel, was 275lb.

In the 1939 Lightweight TT Mellors pushed his 250 to a 3m 45s lead over the German, Kluge, riding a supercharged DKW. It was a brilliant win for Mellors, and a tribute to an elegant, straight-forward, virtually unburstable engine; but Benelli, despite their euphoria, were not blind to the advantages of forced induction. A supercharged version of the single was put in hand, but it was overshadowed by a blown four-cylinder, shown for the first time at the Milan Show of 1939, a matter of weeks before the outbreak of general war in Europe. On the Benelli stand were 250 singles,

supercharged and unsupercharged, and the four. With its Cozette supercharger driven directly from the crankshaft, the single gave 45bhp at 8,800rpm. The four had watercooled cylinders inclined at 15°, hemispherical combustion chambers and 45° valves. The vane-type blower was mounted above the gearbox, ran at half engine speed, and boosted power to 50bhp at 10,000rpm, which, said Benelli's spokesman at Milan, would provide a top speed of 130mph. But war meant that it was never raced.

The works at Pesaro were severely damaged in 1943. Consequently, a couple of years elapsed after the end of the war before Benelli's 250 dohc single was seen again on the race circuits. A road-going 250 had twin cylinders, pushrod-operated valves, and a strikingly smooth exterior for both sides of the crankcase/primary transmission.

Postwar performances in racing, with the 250 single as a staple ingredient, were variable, ranging from a world-championship victory in the 1950 series, with Dario Ambrosini, to much less convincing displays in later years, when Ambrosini's death ushered in an array of other riding talent.

Roadster machines included a 125cc

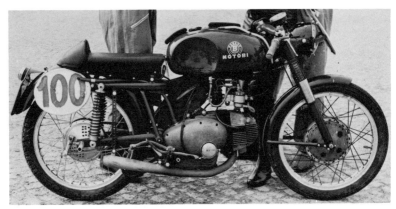

Before De Tomaso stepped in, Benelli entrusted small-machine production to its partner, Motobi. Hallmark of the Motobi line was a horizontal, ohv single-cylinder engine underslung, with in-unit gearbox, from a pressed, beam frame. This is the Sport Special 250 of 1969 having well-oversquare engine dimensions of 74 × 57mm. Power output was 14bhp at 7,500rpm and top speed over 80mph. "Dry" weight was 240lb.

two-stroke single, the Leonico, and an uprated version of the 250 twin two-stroke.

In 1958 the racing single was extensively redesigned. The original bore/stroke of 65 x 75mm was altered to 70 x 64.8mm, twin-spark ignition introduced, and an extra ratio squeezed into the old four-speed gearbox. Weight was cut, through an overwhelming use of light-alloy, from 280lb to 220lb. It was all rather late in the day; a single, no matter how well developed, was by then taking on too much in challenging the high-revving multis. Benelli's multi, when it came in the early 60s, was a fairly conventional transverse four. Bore/stroke were 44 x 49.6mm, figures altered when 350 and 500 versions were called for, as Benelli contested other classes.

It was not until the 1968 season was drawing to a close that the 250 began to show world-beating form. Constant development had brought power up to 50bhp at 16,000rpm, and weight down to 250lb. In 1969 Kelvin Carruthers rode one to win the world championship. Apart from any vagaries in Benelli management and fortunes that might have affected results in 1970, a repeat performance with the four proved to be out of the question when the FIM banned the use of more than two cylinders in 250cc-class racing from the winter of 1969. Enlarged, the four was entered in 350cc races but was unable to match the MV Agustas.

In 1971 Alessandro de Tomaso bought out Benelli and reviewed both the race programme and the roadsters, headed at the time by an attractive 650 vertical twin. Racing was brought to a halt; the roadsters were drastically revised. The 650 was dropped, and a 500 four replacement announced. It was not very far from being a Honda replica. De Tomaso said the Japanese had not been reluctant in the past to copy Europe; now Benelli (and Moto Guzzi) should feel free to reverse the process. More cylinders were added. Benelli's 750 Sei enjoyed press adulation and moderate sales; the same may be said of its later stablemate, the 900. These were the first in a series of multis produced at Pesaro, some of them paralleled by machines in the Guzzi range.

Benelli 650S

In the early 1970s a 650 twin from Pesaro was one of the best-looking of all Italian motor cycles; this is the compiler's opinion, and if occasion to defend it arises he will be happy to do so. A pushrod ohv parallel twin of almost grotesquely oversquare configuration, with side-by-side piston phasing, the 650S had a tipped-forward, rough-finished light-alloy barrel and head on highly polished crank/gear cases, with starter motor and generator mounted to the rear. Contact-breaker ignition was reached through a cover on the crankcase. As was customary a decade or so ago, kickstarter backup was provided for the electric starter. In the Italian way, this took the form of a long, spindly shank incorporating several angled joints to allow it to be tucked to the rear when not in use; the price for this convenience was the necessity for a lengthy, and ultimately uncertain, process to position it for kicking through a restricted arc. However, who would grumble overmuch, if an electrical failure rendered press-button starting inoperative?

The crankcase was split horizontally and held a four-flywheel crankshaft running on no fewer than five bearings. Interestingly, in view of this comprehensive specification, there was a fair amount of vibration and a dearth of "flywheel effect".

Gearbox ratios (selected in '72 by a rightside lever) followed the then usual Italian formula of a high, almost overdrive, top with close spacing of the intermediates — with the exception of bottom, which was very low. In top, 70mph equated to 4,150rpm, 90 to 5,660rpm. Maximum speed was a little disappointing, were credence given to the maker's claims of 57bhp/7,400rpm, for it was almost impossible to exceed 6,000rpm, 96 or thereabouts, on the flat.

The brakes were beautifully executed light-alloy units, the front of 9in diameter, twin-sided, with a rash of stiffening ribs on both plates. The wheels were of

Directed at America, the handsome 650 Benelli, usually advertised as the Tornado, had a 50bhp engine giving a top speed of 105mph.

steep-flanged Borrani type – wire-spoked, of course – carrying Pirelli tyres.

Specification

650S (1972) *Twin-cylinder, ohv, four-stroke. 642cc (82 x 58mm). Five-speed gearbox. 2.9g fuel. Tyres, 3.50 x 18in (fr), 4.00 x 18in (r). 97mph.*

Benelli 250SS

A rare one, this, probably designed specifically for the US market. It had a single-cylinder four-stroke engine arranged horizontally, Aermacchi fashion, with longitudinal finning, and left-mounted, folding kickstarter. Intended for trail and "dirt" use, it was fitted with knobbly tyres, a well-padded, longish single seat and a deep, very "Italian" fuel tank. The engine, with large-capacity oil sump, carried a bolted-up five-speed gearbox. The entire, rather bulky, unit depended from a backbone chassis incorporating pivoted-fork rear suspension; at the front was a conventional telescopic fork.

Power developed, on a 8.5:1 compression ratio, was a claimed 28bhp at 8,200rpm; top speed – another claim – was 95mph.

Specification

250SS (1970) *Single-cylinder, ohv, four-stroke. 250cc (74 x 57mm). Five-speed gearbox. 2.2g fuel. Tyres, 3.50 x 18in. 95mph.*

Benelli 2c 250

"I am firmly against regulations which allow mechanical modifications. Engines should be the same, exactly the same, as those the man in the street can buy. At the TT I saw high-lift cams in machines beautifully prepared – I feel it is wrong. The Benelli 2cs we ran in the Production TT had engines completely standard...of course, there were alterations made to some things, such as restricted steering lock, setback footrests and handlebars. But I did not allow our lads to touch the motors.

"We have, in Italy, a similar engine with 30mm Mikunis capable of about 120mph. Our lads wanted to fit that, but I said No. They were disappointed but if that engine had been used, one

Benelli 250 2C

The 2c was a light, lively 250 that made little impact in 70s markets open to Japanese competition.

machine would not have been a production bike. I would like the ACU to decide just what they will allow, and announce it well in advance of a Production TT race so that everyone will know where they stand."

Who was this man, father-figure to "our lads" in 1975? He was Mr John Durrance, managing director of Agrati Sales, UK concessionaires for Benelli, and he was being interviewed following the entry of a brace of 2c 250 two-strokes in the IoM Production TT.

Val Ward, a two-stroke twin buff, rode the more impressive of the TT Benellis and was immensely impressed....

Both bikes began life as perfectly standard models. To recap, the Benelli 2c has an inclined engine of 56mm x 47mm bore and stroke and a swept volume of 231cc, petroil mixture enters through two 22mm-choke Dellortos, and the transmission, with gear primary drive, incorporates a five-speed gearbox built in unit with the engine.

The exhaust system is unusual, for a modern two-stroke twin, in having a balance pipe between the primary pipes beneath the motor; and ignition is interesting because it is the electronic solid-state type, with two magnetic pick-

ups to fire the coils. For the rest, the Benelli is conventional: duplex cradle frame, telescopic front forks (Marzocchi) and swinging-arm rear suspension, and drum brakes, two at the front.

Verified kerbside weight, including five gallons of petroil, was 314lb. (This was a little lighter than standard, following judicious removal of extraneous bits and pieces.) Compression ratio was 11:1. The comprehensive air-cleaner fitted as standard was detached and the customary 98 main jets were replaced by 108s. Plugs were Champion N-3G.

Ward thought power, in "race" trim, was more, but probably not a lot more, than the 25bhp claimed in the maker's handbook (occurring at 6,870rpm, incidentally, rather than the handbook's quoted 8,670). Tyres were Dunlop TT100; the exhaust system looked ordinary, but Ward suspected a little doctoring to the baffles when he heard the deep note.

Petroil mixture was 20:1 (with Shell 2T) and consumption in the race was about 40mpg.

How did Ward find this inexpensive little racer, with its special 5¼-gallon tank (standard 3g) and beautifully

19

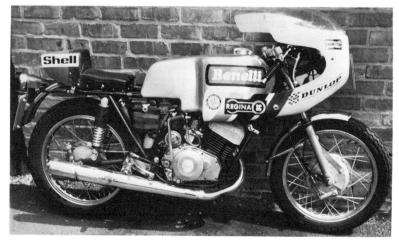

Mildly tuned, the 2c proved a reasonable Production TT machine in the 1975 IoM series.

tailored Lintek fairing and seat? Just fine. No temperament, with a quick warm-up, and an easy cruise within seconds of starting at 50mph at 4,000rpm. "In the lower gears the instantaneous response anywhere between 5,200 and 7,000rpm required great care to avoid over-revving." No vibration...well, perhaps a faint tingle, at high revs.

Steering was spot on, a "revelation".

"The lasting impression is of riding fast velvet...at all times beautifully smooth."

Specification

2c (1975) *Twin-cylinder, two-stroke. 231cc (56 x 47mm). Five-speed gearbox. 3g fuel. Tyres, 3.00 x 18in (fr), 3.50 x 18in (r). 88mph (101mph as production racer).*

Stealing a march on the Japanese – Alessandro De Tomaso's six-cylinder 750 Benelli.

750 Sei: Benelli apologists talked airily of unexceptional width at the crankshaft . . .

Benelli 750 Sei

Alessandro de Tomaso, owner of much of the Italian motor cycle industry, and implacably hostile to the Japanese, was not above carrying the fight to the enemy. Not content with putting up every resistance to the orientals in their European depradations, he retaliated in 1975 with a multi-cylinder superbike that out-Honda'd anything on offer from Japan.

"Multi", in this instance, is a fitting word, for in the mid-70s a six was two pots up on any motor cycle seen on post war roads. Cocking a snook at the Japanese did not end there, for the new Benelli's engine, in layout, specification and appearance, had much more than a passing likeness to the then-current Honda sohc 500-4 – with a couple of extra cylinders tacked on, of course.

At the time, it was reported that the 750 had taken only three years to progress from drawing board to tarmac. The gestation period was so brief that there was talk of Benelli R and D having shown Hammamatsu how to go about its business. In hindsight, there may be some surprise that Benelli took so long. There could have been little development called for in the engine. De Tomaso has spoken of the pleasure it gave him to upset the usual order by commissioning a thoroughgoing copy of a Japanese original.

Weighing under 500lb and having a reasonable (57in) wheelbase, the 750 Sei impressed all who rode it in 1975–76. Smoother (of course) than any of the twins and fours available, it excelled too as a quick-steering motor cycle having taut, responsive handling that belied its power and size.

Three 24mm Dellortos on dual manifolds metered fuel in a restrained way, to give 40–50mpg at 80–85mph, and ignition was by three coils/contact-breakers.

The 750 was followed by a larger version, the 900 Sei, that remains on sale on the continent of Europe in the 80s. In the intervening years, from 1975, the Honda six – which, of course, had to be an original design, for Mr Honda could not be seen to copy a Benelli copy of an earlier Honda – has come, languished, and been declared obsolete.

Benelli 900 Sei

Still sold in Europe (though not in the UK): the 900 Sei. Always underrated, the big Benellis probably suffered through their undeniable Honda connection.

Apart from the big sixes, Benelli multis in De Tomaso's time, all bearing much resemblance to contemporary Hondas, have included 500, 350 and even 250 fours.

Specification

750 Sei (1975) *Six-cylinder, ohc, four-stroke. 748cc (56 x 50.6mm). Five-speed gearbox. 5g fuel. Tyres, 3.50 x 18in (fr), 4.25 x 18in (r). 118mph.*

Bianchi

The lineup of the rival manufacturers in European motor cycle racing at the outbreak of World War II should convince an impartial observer that Italy, in the ingenuity and modernity of its designs, was the paramount nation. Britain had enjoyed most honours during the preceding decade, but remained faithful too long to the outmoded single-cylinder. Germany, with the updated and supercharged BMW twin, was currently top dog. But it was Italy that deserved to take centre stage with designs in advance of anything offered by northern Europe. There were, for example, no fewer than three Italian supercharged fours available: Gilera's 500 Rondine, Benelli's 250, and the Bianchi 500.

The career of all three was cut short by, first, the war and then the decision of the FIM to ban supercharging in postwar racing.

Bianchi's four was a Marco Baldi design. Unlike the other multis, with liquid-cooling, it was air-cooled. The cylinders were set upright, and across the frame, and had close-pitch, shallow finning. Twin overhead camshafts were driven from a vertical shaft on the right, with the cams working directly on valves angled at 90° in hemispherical heads. The supercharger was a Cozette, fitted to the rear of the cylinder block, and the carburettor a Solex. Power output of this advanced 493cc (52 x 58mm) engine was evaluated, in tests conducted by Alberto Ascari, later to achieve greater fame as a racing motorist, at 80bhp at 7,000rpm.

The four represented a peak in the history to that date of Bianchi's involvement in racing, which had begun in earnest in 1924. The firm's beginnings were much older, dating from before the turn of the century. Eduardo Bianchi had made a single-cylinder motor cycle in the 1890s. There had been commendation in the English press for an 8hp model on sale in 1918. (Italy was an ally of Britain in World War I.) In the early 1920s Carletto Maffeis designed and rode 500, later 600, twin-cylinder Bianchis with considerable success.

A 350 single designed by Baldi set Bianchi on the path to racing beyond

Bianchi 175 two-stroke single in the early 50s.

In 1960 Lino Tonti's Bianchi 250 was enlarged to 350cc. This photograph was taken at Imola in June, 1961. Bore and stroke of the six-speed 350 are 65 × 52.5mm. Note the separate camboxes, drive to the rightside cambox being taken from the other. Despite a top speed of some 150mph, the 350 was a disappointment.

Italy. Known as the Blue Arrow, it was in advance of most of its contemporaries. It had twin gear-driven overhead camshafts, a hemispherical combustion chamber and dry-sump lubrication backed by a manually operated system relying on a secondary supply of lubricant stored adjacent to the petrol tank. The compression ratio was 5.5:1, maximum power 20bhp, and top speed almost 90mph. This was fast enough for it to win the 500cc class in the Gran Premio delle Nazioni at Monza, when it beat the likes of AJS (J.H. Simpson up) and Rex-Acme (with Walter Handley). In the Isle of Man, however, at the 1926 TT,

it fared less well, for the Bianchi team finished no better than 13th, 14th and 20th.

The 350 was a force in its class in Europe during the five years up to 1930. It took most of the factory's attention. Sales of road machines were modest and centred on a rather ordinary 175cc single.

Postwar, Bianchi had to rebuild their factory before re-entering the market with 175 singles. One of these, the Tonale, formed the basis for a return to racing, in 1955. Enlarged to 203cc, and with pushrod operation for the oh valves replaced by a chain-driven ohc, the

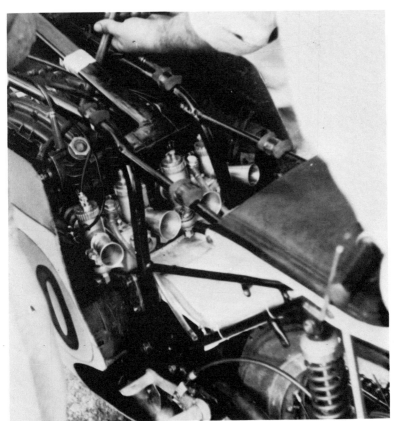

Stretched to the limit, at 450cc, in 1966 the Bianchi twin was equipped with two carburettors per cylinder.

Tonale's engine powered the 250cc-class winner of the Milano–Taranto. With a further capacity increase, to a full 250cc, the single served as a stop-gap racer for Bianchi pending the introduction, in 1960, of Lino Tonti's design for a vertical-twin 250. It had taken only 12 months for the twin to advance from drawing board to race track. Tonti, fully aware of the near-stranglehold exercised by MZ and MV Agusta, had aimed for at least 33bhp and a total weight, with three gallons of fuel, of under 300lb. As first tested, the twin peaked at 34bhp at 11,500rpm and weighed 280lb. Tall and bulky, with a four-bearing crankshaft, four flywheels, and clutch and contact-breaker mounted at opposing extremities of the crankshaft, the engine looked weightier than it was – an impression augmented by the integral 5¼-pint oil sump. Though the engine was mounted in the lowest practicable frame, and its wheels were only 18in, the 250 was noticeably larger, if no heavier, than the established stars in its class. As it was often taken for a 350 in the early weeks of track testing, there was little surprise when Tonti enlarged it, to create a 350cc stable-mate. The change was effected by altering the bore from 55mm to 65mm, while retaining the 52.5mm stroke of the 250.

Both machines were run in the 1960 IoM TT. The results were disastrous. Of

Tonale 175 in the mid-50s.

the six entries in the 250 race, five were forced out, through a variety of failures, leaving Perfetti to finish a lonely ninth. The solitary 350 in the Junior race, ridden by Brambilla, retired during the first lap. The 250 was withdrawn at the end of the season, leaving the 350 to contest 1961 events, mainly in the care of Bob McIntyre and Alistair King. They had a high opinion of the twin, enhanced when early reliability problems were eased with a gentle "de-tuning" operation that lowered maximum rpm from 12,000 to 10,600 but maintained top speed at a competitive 145–150mph.

However, the 1961 season proved a disappointment both for the Scots and their occasional Italian co-rider, Brambilla, and for the factory. From world-championship rounds, Bianchi's tally of places was no better than two seconds, a third and a fourth.

The outcome was a diminution of factory interest. Race entries dwindled. Development lagged. The Japanese arrived to challenge, then oust, MV Agusta, formerly Bianchi's chief rival. In 1967 motor cycle production came to an end at Bianchi of Milan.

Bianchi Tonale 175

At a time – in the 1960s – when the "basic" side of the British motor cycle industry consisted of a mass of two-stroke-engined lightweights, the parallel sector of Italian motor cycling was equally homogeneous. But how much more interesting it seemed! In Italy there was an obsession with racing. Lightweight motor cycles on sale to the public for commuting use were not immune from racing influence. Full springing front and rear, duplex frames, ohc motors in light-alloy with in-unit gears, full-width hubs, and deep, recessed fuel tanks were commonplace

Impressively smooth and quiet, the Tonale Sport of 1961.

on the Italian motor cycle of up to 200cc. All this and, usually, plenty of variegated colours, when British makers remained enamoured of gentlemanly black.

The Tonale 175 fulfilled all the criteria listed above while displaying in extreme form another feature encountered on Italian motor cycles. It had a wildly fluctuating speedometer needle that made it impossible to establish true top speed, while engendering some disbelief in the 90-100mph registered during a spin round the block. Very Latin; most un-Smiths-like.

With a cast-iron barrel and light-alloy head, the Tonale's engine was inclined a degree or two from the vertical. All-enveloping finning gave no clue, on cursory examination, as to the method of valve operation; or even if there were valves at all. In looks, this handsome power unit could have been a two-stroke. In Italy, however, two-strokes were regarded as downmarket scooter power. The Tonale had a single overhead camshaft driven by chain on the right. In the same half of the smooth, bulbous case were the primary chain and large, multi-plate "wet" clutch. Flywheels were full disc, and heavy; the tickover could be slow and very reliable, and there was a reluctance to rev hard. Lubricant was carried in a finned sump. Power developed was claimed to be 8.3bhp at 6,000rpm.

Mechanical noise was subdued – the exhaust note, despite an impressively large silencer, less so. Cruising speed could be around 60mph, about 5mph short of maximum, when rpm were 5,500. Hubs, wheel rims and control levers were in light-alloy but total weight still came out at 340lb. Fuel consumption averaged 90mpg.

Specification
Tonale 175 (1961) *Single-cylinder, ohc, four-stroke. 175cc (60 x 61.8mm). Four-speed gearbox. 3.5g fuel. Tyres, 2.25 x 19in (fr), 2.75 x 19in (r). 64mph.*

Bianchi Bernina 125

At first glance merely a smaller edition of the 175, Bianchi's 125 differed from the Tonale in a number of ways. For one

thing, the valves, while similarly overhead, were actuated by pushrod-operated rockers, the camshaft being at the base of the cylinder, with tunnels for the pushrods at the rear. Primary drive was by helical gears.

In most respects, however, they were much alike. Quiet, extremely economical (the Bernina would return 110mpg at a maintained 30mph), a shade deficient in dualseat padding ... the "family" characteristics were unmistakable, and impressive. *The Motor Cycle*, never a magazine for extravagant word play, summed up the Bernina as being "...one of the most eyeable lightweights. It has a brisk, tireless performance and its economy makes it a fine proposition for everyday use. It is, in a nutshell, excellent value for money."

Exactly, no doubt, the sentiments of Milano's young tearaways of the 60s when they selected a Bernina for traffic banditry.

Specification
Bernina 125 (1964) *Single-cylinder, ohv, four-stroke. 124cc (53 x 56mm). Four-speed gearbox. 3.5g fuel. 2.50 x 18in (fr), 2.75 x 18in (r). 53mph.*

Bimota

Bimota SB4

Most people agree that the outstanding thing about a Bimota is its frame. As this is Italian-made and in 1984 accounted for approximately three-quarters of the total price of £8,000 for an SB4 (powered by a Japanese Suzuki four-cylinder), no further reason needs to be advanced for this entry.

Bimotas are made in a small factory at Rimini. The firm was started in 1975 by three men, Bianchi, Morri and Tamburini, the initial and second letters of their names forming the company's name. In the 1980s a workforce of some 32 produced around 10 models a week. The chassis...frame?; call it what you will...is superb. Its pedigree includes world road-race championships with

A Bimota, with Japanese four-cylinder power, selling at £8,000.

Walter Villa, and Aermacchi/Harley-Davidson, and the Venezuelan Johnny Cecotto, whose 1975 Yamaha was Bimota-framed. It extends forward of the steering head, with massive tubular bracing in the area. There are three basic sections to the frame. An upper section runs back to the rear shock-absorber mountings; there are two plates (machined from a solid billet of a super-light but strong alloy known as Arconal) joining the upper section to the suspension system and rear pivoted fork; finally a lower cradle that can be unbolted for removal of the engine. The frame tubes are in an unexpectedly heavy gauge of chrome-molybdenum; the factory stresses that it is unwilling to risk flexing in the area by saving a few ounces.

The front forks are by Ceriani, to Bimota design, with 40mm stanchions, and have rebound damping adjustment through no fewer than seven settings. The legs are mounted in yokes machined from Arconal and are, interestingly, free of the anti-dive arrangements that have become a commonplace on other, usually slower, machines. Earlier forks, made almost entirely "in house" by Bimota, were more complicated. The top part of the legs on 1980-model frame kits were taken into the steering head, to reduce inertia effect, while the lower part, in the yoke, deviated from the steering head. Bimota's idea was to reduce the effect of geometry change during heavy braking. Adjustable trail was provided by eccentric setting of the bearings.

Frame welding is carried out by the costly and skill-intensive TIG (tungsten inert gas) process, developed to subject metal to least stress while presenting the smoothest appearance.

The wheels are made by Bimota and take tubeless tyres. Replacement cost is in the region of £300 per wheel, a figure probably justified by a lengthy process that includes both riveting and glueing, following forging in Bologna and further work at the MV Agusta helicopter plant. Originally, proprietory (and hardly less expensive) Campagnola wheels were used; Bimota claim that the latest pattern is lighter.

The braking system incorporates the 11in Brembo discs, with twin-piston calipers, found on the majority of present-day high-performance motor cycles in Europe. A standard Suzuki master cylinder is used at the front, along with other stock switchgear from Japanese concerns.

Twin silencers, to Bimota specification, serve four pipes and the favoured tyres are Michelin A/M59s.

The glass-fibre fairing is comprehensive, beautifully made, and attached to the frame by means of rubber bushes. Total weight, "dry", is in the region of 460lb.

Specification

SB4 (1983) *Four-cylinder, dohc, four-stroke. 1075cc (72 x 66mm). Five-speed gearbox. 4.8g fuel. Tyres, 120/80 x 16in (fr), 150/80 x 16in (r). 150mph.*

Cagiva

Cagiva WMX 125

An example of the watercooled motocrosser destined to become commonplace in international racing, this Cagiva was beautifully made and, outside Italy, extremely expensive. It was not, in default of close examination, immediately identifiable as being watercooled, for there were plenty of "cooling" fins on show. The radiator was small and almost concealed by the upward sweep of the exhaust system. Cylinder and head were in rough-finished aluminium, cooled by about two pints of liquid in circulation to half the depth of the barrel and through a myriad of passages in the head.

The six-speed gearbox had a large seven-plate clutch, with a kickstarter operating on the straight-cut gears of the primary drive. Ignition was by a (Japanese) internal-rotor CDI unit.

The tubular frame, in chrome-moly steel, high and well supported around the steering head, had a square-section rear fork controlled by ultra-long spring units. The front forks were credited with 11in travel and appeared to be of Ceriani

Cagiva production moto-crosser; this one, of course, is air-cooled.

manufacture, though "Cagiva" was the name that was cast on the lower legs.

As a rare Italian intruder in a field dominated by the Japanese and manufacturers from northern Europe, the WMX aroused interest but did not perform well enough to overcome the handicap of a retail price 20–30 per cent above that of the "competition".

Specification

WMX 125 (1981) *Single-cylinder, watercooled, two-stroke. 124cc (56 x 50.6mm). Six-speed gearbox. 1.5g fuel. Tyres, 3.00 x 21in (fr), 4.00 x 18in (r).*

Ducati

Most of Ducati's considerable renown derives from the work of Fabio Taglioni, who was made head of design in 1954. It

is, of course, impossible to write or talk of Taglioni without reference to desmodromics; to positive valve control. The principle, as it concerns motor cycles, did not originate with Taglioni: James "Pa" Norton roughed out sketches for a form of desmodromics for his ancient singles in 1909.

Taglioni first developed a desmo cylinder head in 1948, but it was not until he joined Ducati that he found the resources to perfect it. By the 1950s valve springs in four-stroke racing singles were having a rough time; many good judges, Taglioni among them, were sure they were at the limit of useful life.

"Over"-revving can allow valves to contact the piston. The desmodromic system overcomes the problem by closing the valves *precisely*; cams return the valves to their seats as positively as they lift them. In Ducati's first desmo head, fitted to the factory's 125cc racers,

Desmo 125 twin was first raced in 1958. Its 42.5 × 45mm engine produced 22.5bhp, for a top speed of 118mph in sixth gear.

the valves were opened as in a normal overhead twin cam, with one camshaft for the inlet, the other for the exhaust. For closing, however, two odd-shaped cams on a third, middle, shaft controlled the valves via a pair of inverted rocker arms connected by flanged collars to the valve stems. This "closing" shaft was driven by vertical shaft and bevel gears, in the normal way, and in turn drove the ordinary "opening" camshafts through spur gears. The valves were inclined at 80° to each other, being closed to within 0.012in of their seats by desmo action; final sealing was effected by cylinder pressure.

Before Taglioni's arrival, Ducati – set up in 1950 on funds provided jointly by the Italian government and the Vatican – had been content with a straightforward range of commuter machines. The Cucciolo, "little pup", was a 48cc four-stroke having frugal fuel-thirst and useful performance. It was exported to the UK for assembly to road-readiness in a warehouse in north-west London. Being noisy and temperamental, it found a home with English motor cyclists but never laid claim to be considered as better than a mechanical freak. It was

raced at Brands Hatch under the name of Britax and was much favoured by female competitors.

Taglioni's first notable design was a 100cc ohc racer – nicknamed Marianne – which, in 1955, took class victories in the Giro d'Italia and the Milan–Taranto. With a desmo head, and enlarged to 125cc, it was entered for the 1956 Swedish GP. There, in wraparound streamlining, it outran the opposition, revving to 12,500, and occasionally to 14,000, when it attained more than 100mph.

The outstanding performance of the desmo was recorded at the last grand prix of the 1958 season, at Monza, where 125 singles finished first, second, fourth and fifth, with a new Ducati 125 twin in third position; the highest-placed rival was an MV, in sixth place.

While Ducati were racing, their range of road machines was based on four engine sizes – 98, 125, 175 and 204cc. The 125 and 175 were virtually Formula racers, fitted with lights and kickstarters but without the desmo head. Later, in the 1960s, variety was increased. There were 250s, 350s, 450s. Pride of place went to the classic 250 Mach 1. Fitting a

Ing. Taglioni's original desmo Ducati was a 125 single and appeared in 1956. This is a 1958 version producing 20bhp at 13,000rpm (maximum safe revs being 1,000 higher).

Ducati 175 of 62 × 57.8mm, designed by Taglioni in 1956, was raced with success in Formula 3 events. Its top speed, on a 9.5:1 compression ratio, was around 100mph.

Top view of a desmodromic Ducati twin.

Desmo valve-gear enclosure.

34

desmo head to these machines promised to be prohibitively expensive. The advantages of the system, however, were too pressing to be ignored. Taglioni simplified his original layout. Bevel gear and vertical drive remained as before, but the four cams for opening and closing the valves were grouped on a single camshaft. This permitted production costs to be cut, and the system is the one utilised to the present day.

The first "mass-produced" desmo roadsters were released in 1969. With engine options of 250, 350 and 450cc, clip-on handlebars and a generally sporting profile, they were sold in the USA in company with three similar-sized – but desmo-less – "street scramblers".

Honda's 1969 presentation of their 750 four undoubtedly spurred Ducati into pressing ahead with a European 750. Their vee-twin surprised the motor cycling world and delighted a small part of it. The advantages of Taglioni's 90° design were at least threefold. It was more or less vibration-free, as narrow as a single-cylinder, and had unlimited cornering clearance; none of these virtues was to be found in the faster and more luxurious Japanese four.

The vee-twin was not, in fact, Ducati's first venture into big motor cycles. There had been an earlier, and very big, motor cycle: the 1,200cc vee-four Apollo which weighed 600lb and had a power output of more than 100bhp. It was intended to win favour with the buying department for the Italian police but failed to outshine Moto Guzzi's contender, the V7.

Although Ducati withdrew from grand prix racing in the early 1960s there have been occasional forays into lesser competitions, with notable victories in such events as the Barcelona 24 Hours and the Imola six-hour race. The vee-twin, too, has been raced. It scored in the Imola 200, in the hands of Paul Smart and Bruno Spaggiari, and of course a few years later in the Isle of Man, when Mike Hailwood chose a 900SS for his return to racing, and won the 1978 Formula 1 event.

The Italian government is now sole shareholder in nationalised Ducati, following a financial crisis in the mid-70s when it appeared that de Tomaso might add the company to his group.

Ducati 100 Gran Sport

A 1955 newcomer, the 100 Gran Sport was intended for sporting use in events such as the Giro d'Italia. Neatly contrived, it had (of course) an ohc

Monza Junior 160 with 61 × 52.5mm engine in a frame designed for a 250. Ducati expert Alan Cathcart has pointed out that the mudguards are clearly designed for wheels larger than the 160's 16in. This is a 1965 model.

Desmo 350 prepared by John Surtees and photographed at Brands Hatch in 1962.

power unit of 49.4 x 52mm = 100cc which, on a compression ratio of 8.5:1, was reputed to turn out 9bhp at 9,000rpm, to give a road speed of more than 70mph.

The valves were operated by rockers from a single camshaft driven by the usual Ducati arrangement of shaft and bevels.

Specification

100 Gran Sport (1955)   *Single-cylinder, ohc, four-stroke. 100cc (49.4 x 52mm). Four-speed gearbox. 2g fuel. Tyres, 2.50 x 17in. 72mph.*

Ducati 200 Super Sports

People like Charlie Rous, no stranger to high-powered motor cycles, invariably were surprised, then impressed, by a first ride on a small Ducati. Sometime record-breaker on a 1-litre Vincent, Charlie had been a correspondent on motor cycling matters to a Fleet Street daily. It was thus perhaps inevitable that he should fondly publicise the 200SS as

the Bologna Bomb. (But why not Bologna Banger?)

In 1960 no British-made 200 was good for more than 60mph; the 19bhp Ducati would do 80mph without apparent effort; on a downhill run it would reach over 90. Commentators said that it was on a par with a good British 350. The only point at which its small capacity was noticeable was during acceleration, and then only in certain circumstances. In third gear, from 50mph or thereabouts, there could be a sense of labour in overtaking. This was compounded when a pillion passenger was carried. However, this latter situation seldom occurred, for the 200 was not inviting for two people. The dualseat was short and its rear section thin; in any case, carrying a passenger tended to interfere with the typical 200 owner's habit of sliding rearward and using the second set of footrests.

Marzocchi suspension with two-way damping gave good handling and acceptable comfort. The brakes were exceptional, the front one being the larger, at 180mm, and enclosed in a full-width alloy hub with ventilated back plate. Fuel consumption averaged 80–100mpg.

Monza 160 engine.

Specification

200SS (1960) *Single-cylinder, ohc, four-stroke. 203.7cc (67 x 57.8mm). Four-speed gearbox. 3.75g fuel. Tyres, 2.75 x 18in (fr), 3.00 x 18in (r). 82mph.*

Ducati Mach 1

The compiler wrote of the 250 Mach 1 in 1965..."I have obtained 95mph from a roadgoing 250. It was a Ducati Mach 1 and it was fitted with a large silencer that did a decent job. I should be stretching the facts by suggesting that the Mach 1 is unlike a racer: in fact, it is a racer by birth and development, now detuned a little for sale to 'the boys'. It is very like the Ducati works racers of a few years back, before they went desmodromic. The chief difference seems to be that whereas the factory's racers, fitted with

megaphone exhaust systems, required only 175cc to achieve 100mph, the production Mach 1, with its large-capacity (and very efficient) silencer, has had to be boosted to 250cc to manage the ton."

For anybody over 25, riding the Mach 1 on the road is a chastening experience. It makes you feel the scurry of the passing years. Not, I stoutly affirm, because of any discomfort in wrapping *my* ageing limbs around the flanks of this fiery midget; no, it's just that one feels conscious of one's years; dropped bars and a racing seat are, after all, a distinctly teenage thing. But there is another aspect. I read, in a glossy American car magazine, some nostalgic pages devoted to the revivifying joys of motor cycle ownership. Pride of the writer's extensive stable was a Ducati Diana (US name for the Mach 1). Among

Newspaperman Charlie Rous, a comfortable 200 pounds or thereabouts, and more familiar with a British 1,000cc big twin, on a 200SS.

The 200SS in 1964.

the therapeutic benefits he claimed for regular outings on his spindly-tyred iron were immunity from coronary troubles, a clear skin, lively appetite and (I think) fully floating kidneys.

Ironically, the Italian Ducati is a best-selling motor cycle fashioned on the lines of the once-traditional British sporting motor cycle. It is a noisy, thumping single with a strong disinclination to tick over at less than 2,000rpm, and a tendency to vibrate as revs approach the other end of the scale. There are five 250 Ducatis currently in production. The Mach 1 is the top performer and, fittingly, the best-looking, with a beautifully shaped petrol tank which is narrow at the rear,

Mach 1 250 in 1964: near-100mph performance and a "dry" weight of 260lb. Power output was claimed to be 27bhp. Note the breather pipe, as big as a frame tube.

for the knees. It has a cylinder barrel of light-alloy, alluringly finned, with a cast-iron liner; the head is also of alloy, with inserted valve seats. The compression ratio is 10:1 and power output, the handbook claims, 28bhp at the crank at 8,000rpm; much of this power, and the erratic tickover, are derived from the rather extreme valve timing provided by the single race-type camshaft. (Valve overlap is greater than that specified for open-pipe Manx Nortons and some 7R AJSs.) The carburettor is a steeply-inclined, 29mm remote-needle Dellorto.

The gearbox is a five-speeder – all 250 Ducatis are thus equipped – fitted in unit with the engine and driven by helical gears giving 2.5:1 reduction ratio.

Performance is ... surprising. This Ducati will cruise at 75–85mph on a motorway, and the only ill effects are likely to be felt at the rider's neck and shoulders, which have to endure the strains imposed by the narrow, downturned bars and a necessity to maintain forward vision. Sitting up as far as I was able, I found the Mach 1 would

maintain 85mph. Revs at this speed, fifth gear engaged, were about 6,500; an almost immediate speed increase was obtainable by (a) crouching along the tank or (b) engaging fourth gear, when revs would rise to 7,000 and road speed to almost 90mph. Fifth gear, at 5.4:1, is virtually an overdrive, although very close to the 6.11:1 fourth; but the 500rpm differential is critical. On normal roads top gear was almost invariably too high when one was seeking the best possible speed, and a slight headwind on a motorway would knock 10mph off the top-gear range. Up to 7,000rpm there was no vibration to speak of: from 7,000 to 8,000 – quite practicable in second and third gears – it was appreciable, and uncomfortable.

A large-diameter breather pipe in clear plastic, stretching in full view from crankcase to rearmost tip of the rear mudguard, remained unsullied by any trace of interior oil. However, I found, probably in common with most owners, that it contributed powerfully to the "racer" image of the bike. A pointer to

In 1967 the Mach 1 was dropped in favour of the Mach 3 series (there was no Mach 2) which had a strengthened, wider crankcase holding more oil than ever before. At first almost a performance match for the sorely missed Mach 1, this version was progressively "detuned" until, as pictured here, in 1974, its top speed had dropped to about 85mph. Tyres (on Borrani rims) measure 3.50 × 18in rear, 3,00 × 19in front, the front brake is a double sls Grimeca, and the front fork is manufactured by Marzocchi.

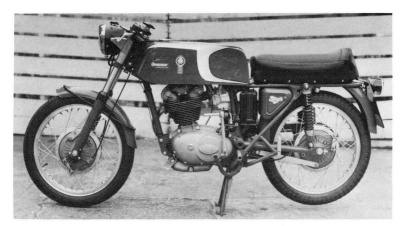

A further 250 variation was the Spanish-made 24 Horas model, built under licence by Mototrans of Barcelona and imported to Britain in 1972-73 by Vic Camp of east London. A (Spanish) Amal carburettor and large, rather unlovely fuel tank helped to distinguish the 24 Horas from the Mach 3.

the unstuffy way in which dealers – and I daresay the makers and concessionaires – look at the Mach 1 was expert advice to "Give it a run in second", were kickstarting to fail. The implication is that Mach 1 owners are quite happy to start their bikes this way, and probably even relish a sprint alongside; it would all be part of that racer image. In fact, there was no trouble in starting it conventionally, once I realised that the carburettor needed plenty of petrol and that the air slide had to be closed if the engine was cold. With all the light-alloy, and the plentiful finning, and the oil reservoir at the base of the crankcase, exposed like an oil-cooler, the Ducati ran cool in all circumstances.

Steering was good, very light of course with the 2.50in section front tyre and the bike's 255lb weight, but the suspension, both ends, was so firm and the seat so unyielding that it was difficult to assess roadholding in any objective way. Road ripples brought the wheels up in a little skip, but there was no shimmying. For years we have been led to believe that excess poundage pilfers speed and comfort. Long ago the low weight and beautiful handling of the

Guzzi racers were linked, and quoted to shame the portly Nortons and other British contenders which turned the scales at TT weigh-ins at 310–315lb. Now I am not so sure.

The gear change was delightful, as were the clutch and brakes. As for fuel consumption, I cannot answer fully for most of my time with the Mach 1 was spent on motorways. Rough checks suggest about 60mpg on premium or super grade, when using all or most of the performance.

Somebody has said the Mach 1 is in every way except cubic capacity a modern equivalent of the pre-war International Norton. I had the experience of being overtaken by a big Velocette while riding at just about full throttle in fifth gear. Perhaps this would not have happened if I had been riding an Inter? What is certain is that I was rather annoyed; and this, when you think about it, is a perverse tribute to the startling power and all-round style of this flyweight roadburner. It can so accustom one to seeing off the majority of other two-wheelers that quite unreasonable disappointment results when another thumping single, of equal breeding but double capacity, refuses to submit.

Specification

Mach 1 (1965) *Single-cylinder, ohc, four-stroke. 248cc (74 × 57.8mm). Five-speed gearbox. 3g fuel. Tyres, 2.50 × 18in (fr), 3.00 × 18in (r). 96mph.*

Ducati Sebring

The Sebring was the 350 tourer in Ducati's range in the late 60s. D.L. Minton had a few days to spare in the November of 1968 and borrowed a Sebring to take him on the classic Land's End–John O'Groats run. Forever an optimist, he was none the less a very experienced motor cyclist and thoughtfully looked out his best Stormgard coat. This proved to be wise, for a downpour appeared to accompany him throughout the 2,089 miles of his journey, ceasing only on those few occasions when snow took over. His notes make interesting reading. They are in part a hymn to the qualitites of the Ducati, at other times a diatribe on, among other disappointing aspects of life on the road in 60s Britain, the state of roadside eating places..."Rain began not half an hour [he writes] after I left home in London for Cornwall, and steadily worsened throughout the trip, but the Sebring motored along quite happily, and so, initially, did I, for the old Stormgard would have kept a man dry under water.

We must have looked an odd pair – the gleaming silver and black Italian lightweight and what must have appeared to be a wet, loosely stuffed bell tent grossly overflowing the seat area. Luckily the Ducati was not one of the sports models for which the factory is so famous; had it been, the ride might have had a very different conclusion. As it was, its low bottom gear and touring riding position were just right."

Later, in Penzance ... "The Ducati required no servicing other than a pint of oil in the sump and oiling of the rear chain. It was covered in mud and spray but not a trace of oil stained the engine/gearbox unit. Now that, coupled with its vibration-free performance, is what endeared it to me. I would be willing to wager that this machine would travel further, with less trouble, than the vast majority of motorcycles. ...On we went, in a manner most undignified for a touring motorcycle but eminently suitable for covering many miles in a short time. I was approaching corners at higher speeds than I was accustomed to and leaving braking till quite late, and in perfect safety, even to the point of braking while cornering. No doubt the modest power output contributed much to this feeling. I found the rear brake exceptionally good; my usual reaction is to leave the rear well alone for most serious braking and to use it as no more

The 350 Sebring as it finished the journey described in these pages.

than a steadying device, but the one on this machine was very good, requiring pretty hard pedal pressure to lock it but being powerful and responsive. The front brake, however, was in a class of its own. Like the Triumph 8in front brake it is a sls device, with none of the fierceness of so many 2ls units. It is as good to look at as it is to use, moreover...so typical of Italian alloy castings.

"The brake holds the speedometer drive: sensible idea, this, as it should contribute to accurate readings, for the cable is short, free from engine oil and rev surges. But, as seems usual on Ducatis, the speedometer itself is a poor instrument. It is completely undamped. Road shocks and engine vibration had as much effect on the position of the needle as did cable revolutions; indeed, while trying for quarter-mile times it was, according to the speedo, possible to obtain 70mph, and no more, in every gear save bottom."

On the long stretches of A1, north of Stamford..."I just sat and thought and watched the rain swirl and bounce in silver splinters along the road, in the headlamp beam. I had time to think of the bike: its saddle and handlebars, exhaust note, lighting, controls, fuel and oil reservoirs, consumption.... As with all Italian seats, this one felt too hard initially, but over a distance of 2,000 miles I never once felt uncomfortable. The exhaust note was too loud and too penetrating, and that is about all that can be said about it: it just should have been quieter. All the controls were light, a pleasure to use – the clutch, especially... The unit itself is of normal multi-plate type but has the great advantage of running in oil. Consequently it was, as far as I could tell, impossible to make it malfunction, despite my slipping it for minutes on end. The oil it runs in, incidentally, lubricates the engine and gearbox also; that is a marvellous idea...no messy external oil pipes, no oil tank, no separate fillers for the gearbox or primary drive."

At this point in his musing Minton experienced a closedown in sparks and lighting. Loose connections, rectified after a scrabble in the wiring loom. On to Edinburgh, and beyond. On the

Precise capacity of the 350 Sebring was 340.2cc, achieved with bore/stroke of 76 × 75mm. Power output was a modest 20bhp at 6,250rpm, giving a top speed of no more than 80mph.

Inverness-to-Wick section, he decided the Sebring was at its best... "Top speed was immaterial, roadholding and braking were of paramount importance. I seriously doubt that any machine could have covered the distance much faster, for though the road was damp we flew along. The gears, with the exception of first, which was too low, were well placed, and close enough to cover all conditions. Top made an excellent cruising gear, though it was not so high as to be an overdrive; the low-speed power of the Ducati allowed it to be brought into use quite early, from 40mph – but, not unnaturally, there was not much acceleration available in this gear at low speeds. I began to wish for more performance, but the snag here is the Sebring's tiny carburettor which, although contributing to good fuel economy and low-speed tractability, strangles any tendency to high revving. For all that, it is a machine capable of breaking the speed limit by at least 15mph and, what's more, cruising at that speed indefinitely and economically."

The only engine characteristic that could possibly be faulted was a shortage of "flywheel"; coupled with the high compression ratio, this meant that if the revs were allowed to drop too low the engine would stall, unless free of load.

After a further bout of electrical trouble, on the windswept reaches of the Devil's Elbow, he was on his way south, averaging 63.1mpg, touching 85mph on occasion, and ending the run full of enthusiasm for the lightweight (270lb) Ducati.

No run-round-the-block tester, this Minton fellow.

Specification

Sebring (1968) *Single-cylinder, ohc, four-stroke. 340cc (76 x 75mm). Five-speed gearbox. 2½g fuel. Tyres, 2.75 x 18in (fr), 3.00 x 18in (r). 85mph.*

Mick Walker Ducati 350

If "amateur" racing is your weakness, what would you say to a lightweight 350 capable of 120mph and selling for £685 (including VAT)? Such a machine was offered by the race-dealer Mick Walker in 1973, and made more than a few clubmen happy. M.R. Wigan tried one in June of that year....

"The machine is basically a specially designed frame housing a mildly-tuned 350 road engine. The normal front brake is either a Grimeca or a Spondon unit.

"The specification to which it is built could have been achieved in 1965, before Yamahas became dominant in production racing. This is rather sad because the performance available puts the Ducati on a par with the Aermacchis, Nortons and AJSs that set the pace in the 70s.

"The test was carried out at Silverstone under overcast skies and with damp patches on the track. At first sight, the Ducati appeared slim, low and long: the sort of bike that you sit in rather than on, with everything tucked away to

Testing the Mick Walker 350 Ducati.

make the most of the narrow cross-section and already generous ground clearance. The exhaust system is slung underneath, and emerges on the side opposed to the final-drive sprocket. The front forks are Ceriani, the front brake a Fontana (replacement for the usual Grimeca or Spondon) and the rear a Ducati-made unit. The frame is of the spine variety, made from T45 tubing, with a number of subsidiary tubes, sections and junctions that look a little untidy on this (pilot) model. Steering-head bearings are taper-roller, with needle rollers at the swing-arm pivot. The steering head is effectively supported by multiple rails at top and bottom of the stem, and overall torsional stiffness should be considerably greater than that of the rather flexible standard Ducati layout."

The test beginning, Wigan found that the 350 wasn't a very eager starter; the 38mm carburettor required "firm treatment" and only with the help of dedicated pushing from a sturdy assistant was he able to get away. This was on the first occasion; thereafter, apparently, the motor was a certain, easy starter. The production 350 Walker Ducati was offered with a 35mm carburettor, which would have made for a more tractable motor. Special equipment on this version included Smiths or Krober rev-counter, Tommaselli levers and clip-ons and Girling rear spring units.

On the track, handling was exemplary ... and "the steering better than on almost all the machines that would have been praised as being exceptionally good only four or five years earlier".

Summing up, Wigan described the Ducati thus: "Solid and stable, with a deceptively lazy style of progress: absolutely ideal for a beginner on any circuit, and excellently suited to the long road races in Ireland or the Isle of Man."

Specification

Walker Ducati 350 (1973) *Single-cylinder, ohc, four-stroke. 340cc (76 x 75mm). Five-speed gearbox. 4g fuel. Tyres, 2.75 x 18in (fr), 3.00 x 18in (r). 120mph.*

Ducati 750 SS

The core of the desmo 750SS, introduced in 1974 and now rated as the most desirable of all Ducatis, is, of course, the engine. An "exploded" diagram shows its elegant simplicity. The bottom-end was as for the conventional (i.e., sohc) 750 Ducati, with a special camshaft, while the pistons, heads, cams and valve gear were all designed especially for the SS.

Desmodromic valve operation looks deceptively simple as laid out Ducati style. The cam form has two separate ramps for each valve, and the valve itself has a lower rocker collet held in position by two half-circle lengths of wire. One cam opens the valve – the other closes it. The closing clearance is zero and the top clearance 5 thou. The cam profiles are obviously material for very precise grinding and hardening. It is a tribute to Ducati that – after the first 1,000 miles of settling-in – valve clearances remained virtually unaltered for thousands of miles, which made the desmo a perfectly practical road machine.

The cams are timed and driven by bevel gears. The shaft is split by a stepped section covered by a sleeve. This allowed the compression ratio to be adjusted easily, and the heads to be removed and replaced without problems.

M.R. Wigan, a Ducati convert (from Japanese hardware), toured and raced a 750SS and describes some of the maintenance work involved in desmo ownership.... "The heads have to be removed to reset tappet clearances and, like the Honda CR93, this means removing the engine. Also, like the CR93, this is a matter of undoing three bolts; it is just that the sheer weight of the engine and the tightening of the fit in the frame makes this a three-handed job. Be warned!"

The front head can be removed with the engine in situ but although theory suggests that the same should apply in the case of the rear head, Wigan never quite managed to do so. Squish-band clearance can go down to 40 thou (1mm), so there is a fair margin left in most 750s as they are delivered.

While most of the engine is a delight, there are *some* shortcomings. The oil-filtration system is a single gravel-straining tube of gauze; the kickstarter has a poor spline location; and the two foot controls both have an unreasonable amount of slop built in.

As a road machine, the SS is poorly finished when compared with some of the "opposition". The picture changes

First 750 Sport appeared in 1972. With yellow tank and panels and single seat (double optional), it had striking looks and performance to match. Top power was 56bhp, at 8,200rpm, and top speed 125-128mph.

Next step for Ducati, in 1973, was to uprate a Sport's performance by fitting desmo valve control. In this form the Sport became Super Sport and gained 10bhp and 10mph. Race-shop assembled, the engine could be run up to 9,000rpm.

within 15 seconds of actually beginning to ride the SS. It is simply magical [Wigan's words] in the manner in which it reaches out for the next section of road, and then proceeds to "demolish" it. The spread of torque makes this long and lazy-steering motor cycle positively enjoyable to ride in heavy traffic. The steering lock is restricted, and this can cause no little irritation at times, but the ability to accelerate instantly, in any gear at any speed, more than makes up for this. The SS is slim and can be placed to a hairsbreadth on road or track. Competition, or at least performance-orientated, machines often suffer from lousy idling – they are prone to stall and buck along in stop-start traffic. Here the 750SS is quite superb. The tickover is steady and totally reliable at below 500rpm, and the torque, even at this rate, is enough to avoid those snorting, high-compression-induced stalls so common with other hotstuff machinery used in this way.

Timing requires a neat but expensive timing tool; Wigan found it a "heartbreakingly difficult" exercise. The Ducati points and condensers operate, but hardly "work". Ten degrees static (38° fully advanced), not 12 thou, is the vital datum. The desmo starts easily, in totally standard form, although the tendency for the kickstarter spline grip to slacken is a drawback. Once the machine is in motion, the kickstarter all too frequently swings out and sticks at right angles – infuriating, especially as the lower end of the kickstarter forging is easily chamfered in hard cornering, and highlighting the ground-clearance dangers of leaving the kickstarter in this position while one is riding.

While the gearbox is good, the way in which the operating linkages acquire slop is definitely bad. The same stricture applies to the rod-operated rear disc brake master cylinder connections. The normal Ducati practice is followed: an outrigger selector mechanism is linked to an internal gearbox by a rod. The clutch is rather heavy. Pending the availability of highly desirable anti-lock units, Wigan believed that the Ducati had brakes "to match anything which might otherwise be available".

The SS was tractable and economical. On one occasion Wigan managed a rush hour trip of 45 minutes on less than two-thirds of a gallon of fuel. The exhaust system – unfortunately, in his view – fitted the "racy" image. The Conti "megaphone"-type silencers fitted as standard were quieter only than the works optional high-level exhaust system (with no baffles and no silencers at all). To civilise the note, Wigan fitted "860" silencers. These did not reduce performance significantly but produced a vast diminution in noise level.

It is interesting that Ducati have no great regard for tradition: in all their gleaming modern plant at Bologna in the 70s there was preserved no single example of the amazing machines produced during the preceding decades. The 750SS had barely started its development when the 860 described elsewhere was settled on as the standard big Ducati engine size. However, it has to be said that many design improvements followed that change, not least the use of an outrigger bearing plate to locate the crank and cam bevel drives more precisely, an oil filter which actually worked, and electronic ignition, albeit based on the none-too-efficient Ducati generator.

Specification

Ducati 750SS (1974–76) *Twin-cylinder, ohc (desmo), four-stroke. 748cc (80 × 74.4mm). Five-speed gearbox. 3g fuel. Tyres, 3.25 × 18in (fr), 4.00 × 18in (r). 130mph.*

Ducati GT/GTS 860

After racing the desmo 750 in 1974, Ducati put the lessons of the year to good effect in the design of the 1975 860. "Simple as that," wrote one observer, D.L. Minton.

He had other things to say, of course. Instead of turning out as a compromise, the steering geometry, frame and suspension were to near-race standards... "The 860 is really a full-blooded racing chassis wrapped round a monstrously torquey, softly tuned power unit, topped by boulevard cruiser essentials. The suspension is so hard

The 1975 GT 860, with bodywork designed by Giugiaro and square-cut crankcase covers, has little of the dynamism of the sporting 750s.

Transistorised electronic ignition replaced earlier, unreliable points system.

that, if the road is bumpy, your first ride round the block is going to chatter your teeth. But out of town anybody with an ounce of brain is going to realise just how worthwhile it all is. At high speed the 860 is so good it is almost beyond description. 100mph feels like 60 on lesser machinery, and the 860 sticks to its line like a skate through ice, without the slightest deviation."

Early 860s were available with or without an electric starter. Minton made the point that the premium charged for the starter was well worth while, for the kickstarter provided was too short, low geared and generally insubstantial to be anything but a pain – sometimes literally – to use. Starting, he declared with a wealth of feeling, was "more a matter of luck or boiling rages than design".

When the GTS came on the scene, about 18 months later, the electric starter had become a standard fitting. Unfortunately, firing up one of these big twins was still not free of trauma. It was not, by any means, a matter of turning the ignition key and pressing the button...as had been the practice for many years with the despised UJM (Universal Japanese Motorcycle), as unkind critics pointed out. No, electric starter notwithstanding, there was a ritual to be followed. First, fuel taps had to be switched on. (For any deserter from the ranks of UJM users, this was not necessarily an obvious first step, for several Japanese models by the late 70s were fitted with a permanently "on" fuel supply.) Then the twistgrip had to be firmly rolled open, and closed, to have the accelerator pumps squirt priming fuel into the manifold. Third, the ignition was switched on. Fourth, the twistgrip was eased open by about 20 per cent. Fifth, the starter button was pressed. Finally – and this called for skill, or practice – the choke lever had to be progressively lifted (activating the cold-start device in the carburettors) while the engine was turning. With luck, it would fire and settle into a satisfying, throbby, fast tickover; if luck was not with you, or there had been some blurring of the routine, there was nothing for it but to start again, at approximately stage four.

Compared with the first series, the GTS displayed some other changes, apart from the starting arrangements. Not all were for the better. Where previously, for instance, the headlamp brackets had been solidly made pressings, the GTS contrived bent – albeit chrome-plated – wire, with similar supports for the turn signals. Hose clips held the speedometer and rev-counter on their sockets. The dualseat had been thinned, and a rugged extension of the rear frame, doubling as a grab rail for use by the pillion passenger, had been dispensed with. The switchgear had not been altered. This could not be rated a virtue, however, in view of early criticisms directed at under-sizing, lack of "feel" and labelling, and generally mediocre design. The instruments were made by Smiths of the UK.

Changes that had wrought a definite improvement were mainly internal. Perhaps the most important of these concerned the electronic ignition pack. Previously – as long-term owners found, but testers for magazines never did, owing to the brief duration of bike loans to the press – the ignition would, usually at some highly inconvenient time, simply stop functioning. It did so because of voltage surges created by the impulse generator at high engine speeds, leading to a burnt-out system.

The GTS ignition pack overcame the problem with a transistorised voltage control unit to regulate impulse generator output at high rpm. Additionally, the starter button was taken through a relay instead of carrying the entire load itself.

The rear sub-frame had been lowered by over an inch; this, with the effect of the thinner seat, meant that the riding position was noticeably lower than on the earlier model.

Basically, however, the vee-twin Ducati, officially in "sports-touring" guise, remained what it had been from its inception – a competitive motor cycle. In Minton's words: "A racer distilled by years of grands prix and more years of straining endurance racing. A racer deliberately blunted, rewrought to make it usable on the road, muffled by gentle camshafts and large silencers, shackled by the weight of luxuries, but a racer for all that. One that only the Italians could build."

As might be expected, the crankcase was vertically split. The gears of the valve-drive mechanism were disposed, in the manner of a British single, in a timing case on the right. On the end of the crankshaft, itself a beautifully engineered component, built up, pressed and bolted together and running on large ball-bearing races, with a caged needle-roller big end, was a single bevel gear driving the two shaft gears through right angles. The shafts ran in ball races and transmitted power through bevels to the single camshaft in each head. Clearance was effected by screw and locking nut.

Such engineering does not, of course, come cheaply, or lend itself to mass

Rear-chain adjustment is by eccentric setting of the rear-fork pivot. The kickstarter could be appreciated when low temperatures enfeebled the electric starter.

Single-disc front brake of the GT 860.

production. If ever there was a motor cycle which impressed as the brainchild of an exceptionally talented engineer, this (with others in the Ducati range) was it. Despite the heavy mass of metal in reciprocating motion, the GT/GTS engine was a quiet runner, with the "frou-frou" of the valve train as its most noticeable characteristic ... just the sort of noise that enthusiasts had come to associate over the years with well-brought up cammy engines.

Specification

GT/GTS 860 (1974–76) *Twin-cylinder, ohc, four-stroke. 864cc (86 x 74.4mm). Five-speed gearbox. 4g fuel. Tyres, 3.50 x 18in (fr), 4.00 x 18in (r). 118mph.*

Ducati
Hailwood Replica

You do not have to be a deductive genius to fathom why the Hailwood Replica is so named. In 1978 Mike Hailwood returned to the Isle of Man after a 12-year layoff and won the F1 race on a 900SS Ducati at 108.51mph. The Hailwood Replica was the year-later, natural, commercial result. However, it may be as well to point out, for the benefit of OED pedants with a taste for speed – and in fairness to the Sports Motorcycles team which laboured mightily to improve a standard SS for Hailwood's winning purpose – that an as-bought HR is not a replica in the sense of having an engine, and everything else, precisely in the image of the original. What it is, is a nicely contrived sports bike, complete with race-style fairing, screen and general impedimenta, that has much more than a passing resemblance to Hailwood's racer (while being, comparatively, a little wanting in performance). It was made in Bologna as a batch of 200 for export to the UK.

Apart from the fairing, usually in red and green, with white lining, to match the tank finish, there were few changes from

A 1982 version of the 900SS with cast-alloy wheels and dualseat.

An enlarged 750SS, the 900 Super Sport combined 860 engine dimensions with the high revs potential provided by desmo heads. Maximum power was 79bhp, which could propel the slimline 430lb SS at a timed 140mph. Pictured is an early, 1980 example.

the 900SS. The wheels were to a different design, with a more open look, and anodised gold; the brake calipers had been modified, though not in an obvious way (and mainly, it was said, to save weight). Where the ordinary SS was equipped with old-style Veglia instruments, the HR had Nippon Denso clocks and switches in the console. Fuel-tank size was up a little, at 5 gallons. The only other change was a lengthening of the rear shock absorbers to meet the extra weight of the fairing, tank and rearward disposition of the rider.

Specification

Hailwood Replica (1980) *Twin-cylinder, ohc (desmo), four-stroke. 864cc (86 x 74.4mm). Five-speed gearbox. 5g fuel. Tyres, 3.50 x 18in (fr), 4.10 x 18in (r). 130mph.*

Ducati Darmah

The Darmah came along in 1977. With it Ducati hoped to win over those big-twin enthusiasts who, deterred by the less appealing aspects of Italian workmanship (mainly the doubtful quality of small but vital ancillaries), had drawn back from purchase of the GT/GTS 860 series.

The Darmah was relieved of Aprilia electrical gear in favour of West German Bosch; the small, and not particularly accurate, Veglia instruments were replaced by larger, Japanese-made clocks; the switchgear was comprehensively improved.

UK sales of Ducatis picked up. By 1980 the Darmah had lost its kickstarter. For the first time a Ducati owner was totally reliant on electric starting (or run-and-bump). The silencers were replaced by a more attractive design.

The SD Darmah was fitted with a desmodromic-valve engine: SD for "sports desmo". Of the same capacity as that in the 900SS, it was built to a tamer specification, with a lower compression ratio, thorough air-filtration (where the 900SS had nothing more effective than wire mesh in the intake), and the handsome, but power-sapping, silencers already noted.

Marzocchi suspension front and rear followed the style set by the 860 series, and performed equally well. The frame was altered in detail and proved entirely adequate, if not attaining the standard of the 900SS layout.

In only one area was it possible to say with some finality that there had been

The SD Darmah, styled by Tartarini, as seen during its UK launch in 1977.

little improvement. Exhausted by their labours in pursuit of excellence in the motor cycling essentials ... in engine, transmission, handling ... Ducati folk maintained a traditional Italian disregard

Darmah wheels are by Campagnolo, brakes by Brembo.

for finish quality. One forthright observer, Jim Lindsay, described a Darmah thus: "The finish is appalling. Even after a thorough clean-up the bike looked about two years old rather than the same-year machine it was, with 3,000 on the clock. Bad, bad news. The list: poor chroming on the exhausts and mudguards, more bloom than you'll see in Springtime Spalding on the gas tank paintwork, rust on the frame tubes in several places and unsightly corrosion on the crankcase castings. Ain't good enough for a cycle that'll cost you in the region of two and a half Gs to put on the road."

Specification

Darmah SD (1977) *Vee-twin-cylinder, ohc, four-stroke. 864cc (86 x 74mm). Five-speed gearbox. 4.2g fuel. Tyres, 3.50 x 18in (fr), 4.25 x 18in (r). 110mph.*

Ducati Desmo Sport

In the early 1970s Fabio Taglioni, whose title at the State-financed Ducati concern was, simply, the Director, was overruled by the board of directors in the crucial matter of what sort of 500cc twin was to be produced as back-up to the big vee-twins. The Japanese were making inroads into Italy's home-market sales and counter measures were called for.

Later, the Darmah lost its kickstarter, and acquired a more comfortable, though less elegant dualseat.

Ducati 500 Desmo Sport. Handsome, and fast; yet a disappointing performer.

At Ducati the existing 750s, however they might be modified, were seen as being too large, and expensive, to serve the purpose.

Taglioni offered a 500 vee-twin. He promised that it would be 100lb lighter than the 750s and almost as fast. He was not ignored, for that is not the Italian way. Days of dispute ended in a tactical withdrawal by Taglioni: the new project, for a *parallel*-twin 500, would be the responsibility of a design team that had previously worked under the great man's direction.

The result, visually, was extremely attractive – a trim, smallish middleweight having a shapely, well-finned engine inclined in a neat duplex frame. Unfortunately, apart from its good looks the 500 was, in most practical ways, a disaster. As first laid out, it vibrated badly and there was nothing for it but to undertake a redesign, for inclusion of balance cranks. With these in place, the resultant power loss was so severe that the bike's rakish looks and Ducati's good name looked set to become a laughing matter. Out came the balancers; more design work; the cranks were modified, and replaced, for a marginal improvement. Designer Tartarini of Italjet was called in to help. He made further changes. The 500 was put into limited production – as it turned out, for a very

At a time (1977) when the Darmah series was being equipped with Japanese-made instruments, the 500 had a Veglia display.

limited period. Dr Taglioni, waiting in the wings, was reinstated as chief designer – what is the Italian for "I told you so"? – and unrolled his vee-twin plans afresh, to muted acclaim and the shuffling of Italian footwear in an overspill of egg from a dozen faces.

Pending the arrival of Taglioni's 500, a few of the parallel twins (mostly produced at the Italjet works) were released for export. In the form in which they were sold in the UK, the 180° twins suffered from a forbiddingly high price that clouded the advantages of their desmodromic four-valve heads, ultra-oversquare bore/stroke, rear-set foot-rests and Paioli suspension. Vibration was still considerable, finish of variable quality, and performance, while entrancing Italophile owners who had parted with more than £1,700 (in 1978 the price of a Japanese 1000), was a few mph short of being convincing.

Specification

500 Desmo Sport (1977–78) *Twin-cylinder, ohc, four-stroke. 497cc (78 x 58mm). Five-speed gearbox. 2.5g fuel. Tyres, 3.25 x 18in (fr), 3.50 x 18in (r). 106mph.*

Ducati Pantah

First shown in Italy in 1977, then in successive years at Cologne and Earls Court, the Pantah had acquired a sizable, all-knowing following among the owners of the existing vee-twins long before it was exposed to public gaze. Not for them reliance on the best efforts

Originally designed as a 74 × 58mm 500, the Pantah was enlarged in 1981 to 583cc, on a bore of 80mm. Power developed is 58bhp, giving a top speed of 125mph.

of the motor cycling press; in the months before the official unveiling no self-respecting Ducati club member appeared to be without his own information channel direct from the heart of Ducati Mechanica. Clearly, in its 90° configuration the work of Dr Taglioni, the vee-twin 500 was light, spare and beguiling. It was, most Ducati people averred, the best-looking Ducati ever made; which meant, of course, that for them it was the most attractive motor cycle of all time.

The frame followed traditional Ducati lines in being composed mainly of four horizontal tubes, braced by cross members, from which the engine depended. A DOC member, P.J. Fisher, bought one of the first Pantahs imported into the UK, in early 1980, and found the specification very impressive: "The lower pair of horizontal tubes run along the top of the crankcases. If the lower rear part of the frame appears to be lacking in strength, it is because none is needed at this point; the pivoted fork swings not from frame lugs but from a boss on the back of the crankcases, in bushes continuously lubricated by the oil from the engine – and are, therefore, expected to last indefinitely. Frame stresses are transmitted from crank-cases to frame at three widely separated points on each side. A substantial set of chain-adjusters, with alloy clamps, as used on the 900SS, give extra rigidity at the wheel spindle."

Fisher consulted Ron Williams, of the specialist Maxton frame-building concern, who pointed out ways in which the Pantah's frame could be improved, but then admitted that some commend-able aspects of the existing design would be impaired by any stiffening; notably access to such vital components as carburettors, exhaust pipes and rockers.

Fisher concluded: "Any motorcycle is a mass of compromises, and Ducati have achieved both an exceptionally rigid frame structure and a high degree of accessibility. It would hardly be worth sacrificing the latter for a small enhancement of the former."

What made the Pantah immediately different from other Ducatis was the construction, and appearance, of the camshaft drive. No more of traditional shaft and bevels; this was to be a mid-70s design, and a chain was to take over the job ... not a steel pin and roller affair, awash in lubricant, as might have been expected, but a Fiat-style belt.

Fisher was familiar with the layout long before he took delivery of his Pantah. He described it for the world beyond the limits of the Ducati Owners Club....

Another, non-owner's, view on the finish quality: "The Pantah's beauty is not merely skin-deep. A very high standard of finish is evident, from welding neatness and paintwork to the sparkling shine of the motor's alloy covers."

Specification

Pantah (1980) *Twin-cylinder, ohc, four-stroke. 499cc (74 x 58mm). Five-speed gearbox. 4g fuel. Tyres, 3.25 x 18in (fr), 3.50 x 18in (r). 120mph.*

FB

FB Mondial

In 1950 most 125s in the UK were hard-pressed to get up to 55mph. Imagine, then, the sensation created by the Mondials racing in the Ulster Grand Prix that year: they were reaching 90mph on the straights, and shaming more than a few (mainly British) 250s. Carlo Ubbiali on a Mondial won his Ulster class at 77.46mph, with a fastest lap at just under 80mph.

The 125cc FB Mondial was a dohc single. It was designed by Alfonso Drusiani whose services had been enlisted by the brothers Boselli (Fratelli Boselli = FB) when they decided to make over their concern, previously involved in the manufacture of commercial three-wheelers, to motor cycle production. This was in 1947; and the first motor cycles to emerge from FB's factory at Milan were called Mondials. Like all subsequent machines to bear the name they were lightweights. None was particularly inspired, or inspiring; all were remarkably efficient. They brought together the best aspects of Italian motor cycle practice. Bore of the 125 was 53mm, stroke 56mm, and the valves, angled at 40°, were operated by twin overhead camshafts. The vertical shaft and bevels were enclosed within the generous finning of head and barrel. Hairpin valve springs protruded from the large cambox. Gears took primary power to a four-speed gearbox. Lubricant for the dry-sump system was carried, Guzzi-style, in a container on top of the fuel tank. Power, with the engine running on a 9.7:1 compression ratio, was said to be 12bhp at 9,000rpm.

Very few changes were made to this excellent design from 1948 to 1952. There seemed to be little point: Drusiani's engines were invariably successful when matched against "home" opposition in national race meetings. One idiosyncratic feature was the company's devotion to the old-fashioned girder front fork, at a time when most other makes were turning to telescopics. The Mondial's fork was simple in the extreme, having a single central spring and a profound lack of damping. Rear suspension, too, was hardly an example of innovative thinking, consisting of nothing more than primitive twin plungers as pioneered a decade earlier by Norton. However, the layout, at both ends, was light and troublefree...if somewhat unaccommodating of a rider's comfort...and the Bosellis, with Drusiani, saw no reason to change a winning hand. Where they did strike a blow for modernity was in introducing a measure of streamlining for their racing machines as early as 1949. A year later the streamlining was far more extensive. The front fairing was similar to that favoured

Tarquinio Provini on his works 125 Mondial at the 1956 Dutch TT. Full dustbin front fairing plus tailored rear end gave a speed bonus of several miles per hour.

on 1980s racers, leaving the front wheel exposed but running much higher, with "windows" to the front and side, and enclosing the rider's arms. In addition, the rest of the bike was almost totally enclosed.

Carlo Ubbiali making himself small – and scarce – on a Mondial in the 1951 IoM 125 TT. He finished the year as world champion, the first of many similar titles he was to hold – when MV-mounted – during the decade.

Outside Monza autodrome Mondials were usually raced naked. They were equipped with both front and rear footrests, the latter enabling the rider to adopt a more effective, wind-cheating crouch on the straights. One consequence was that the gear-change lever, pivoting on the hanger for a front rest, had to be extended for use when the rider was balanced on the rear set. Later the rear rests were attached to the mudguard, which meant that the rider could stretch out almost prone. In 1952 the 125 was peaking at 10,000rpm, for 15bhp, on a compression ratio of 10.5:1, and top speed was in the mid-90s.

Although triumphant at its Isle of Man début in 1951 the 125 Mondial was beginning to show a lack of development work. In 1952 Ubbiali lost his world title to MV Agusta-mounted Cecil Sandford, and the works machines, in their original form, were retired. Later they formed the basis of a series of over-the-counter racers and sports models with a sohc in place of twin camshafts.

Roadster design during the honeymoon racer period was not very enterprising. Perhaps the most interesting of the road machines was

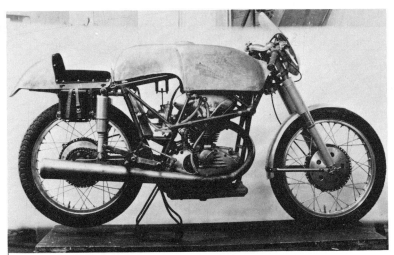

Ready for 1957, the dohc Mondial acquired a trellis of additional frame tubes. Race-long ignition power is stored in the tacked-on battery under the seat.

This 125 Mondial was ridden by Cecil Sandford to a Mellano Trophy win at Silverstone in 1956. Fired by twin plugs, the engine had 53 × 56mm dimensions and drove through a five-speed gearbox.

In 1955 Mondial brought out a racing 250 twin, based on a double-up of the existing 125 single. It was not particularly successful.

a 160cc two-stroke scooter fitted with an ahead-of-its-time electric starter. Attractively styled, the scooter had an elongated crankcase stretching rearward to encase primary trans-

mission, four-speed gearbox, generator and starter motor, and forming also the fork carrying the rear wheel. Thus the engine, transmission and rear wheel created a sub-assembly pivoting under the control of two telescopic shock absorbers.

In racing, by the mid-50s Mondial had come fully up to date, in chassis/suspension terms, with duplex cradle frames, leading-link front forks and a pivoted rear fork. The power units, too, had been greatly modified, and enlarged to take in 175 and 250cc class competition. For the 125 there was a change to wet-sump lubrication, and numerous detail modifications that contributed to an impressive 17bhp and a top speed, when the bike was hidden under a "dustbin" fairing, of more than 105mph. Top Mondial riders of the time, and for long after, were Tarquinio Provini and Remo Venturi.

A five-speed gear box and battery coil ignition were among the features introduced on the 175cc racer and incorporated, by 1956, in the 125's specification. This was a time when Mondial looked set to take a leaf out of

Tarquinio Provini's 1957 world-title-winning 250 Mondial single (or one very like it) was acquired by Stan Hailwood to launch his son, Mike, on a scintillating second year of racing, in 1959, during which he won a string of events leading to the British 250 championship and figured high in international grand-prix ratings. Weighing no more than 220lb, the dohc (75 × 56.4mm) 250 developed 29bhp and had a top speed of 137mph.

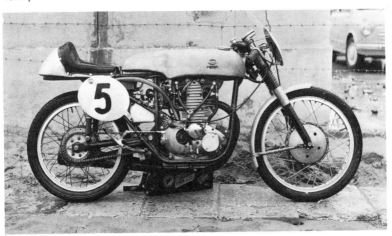

The keen-eyed may be able to detect that the tank name on this 1958 racer is Mondial Paton. When Mondial withdrew from racing in 1957, Giuseppe Pattoni bought a quantity of Mondial components and several partially dismantled machines. First fruit of his rebuilding labours was this dohc 175.

Standard 175 Mondial in the mid-50s had dohc and full springing.

In 1956 a sports version had modified forks, full-width hubs and hump-backed seat, while retaining unusual far-forward position for the kickstarter.

Giulio Carcano's book, at Moto Guzzi, in the field of chassis design. Experiments were carried out with a trellis layout, in the search for extra rigidity, but in final 1957 form the 125 had a conventional duplex cradle braced by extra struts running from steering head to crankcase. Enclosed in a superbly streamlined "egg", the 125, Provini up, lapped Monza in 2 minutes 5.4 seconds during 1957 GP practice; this time was not beaten until 1964.

In 1957 the FIM banned streamlining in grand prix racing and Mondial, along with Guzzi and Gilera, pulled out. Had the firm continued racing it is likely that Mondial engines would have had their valves controlled by desmodromics, for much work had been done to this end at the Milan factory. The Mondial design was quite straightforward, though very different from Dr Taglioni's system devised for Ducati at about this time. There were four camshafts – two for valve lift, two for positive closure – operated by a train of gears running in inverted "L" formation on the left side of the engine.

No 250 twin was ever raced.

When Mondials first looked at the 250cc class they were undecided between multi or single; in the event, a single was enlarged to 250cc (as mentioned earlier) and then, as "insurance", a twin was developed. It was essentially a double-up of the GP 125, and none the worse for it, giving around 35bhp at 10,000rpm, though the total weight of the bike came as a disappointment, at close to 400lb.

The single, with five-speed gearbox (a seven-speeder was a later option) and dual ignition, developed 29bhp at 10,800rpm. It was built in the Carcano mould of a relatively low powered motor for a slippery, lightweight motor cycle having superlative handling. With dustbin fairing, the 250 Mondial in 1957 proved able to better lap times set by unfaired 500s no more than three years earlier.

After Mondials withdrew from racing, ex-works machines were seen in many unfamiliar places, both in Italy and abroad. Some formed the basis of Paton's first racers; others came to Britain, where one was ridden to good effect by the young Mike Hailwood.

Garelli

The first Garelli, built by Adalberto of that name, appeared in 1913. It was a 350cc split-single two-stroke, and something of a masterpiece. Both cylinders were cast in one block and had a common combustion chamber. Cooling was aided by an air vent arranged between

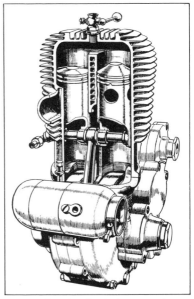

The 350 Garelli split-single two-stroke.

Adalberto Garelli on his 350 in 1914.

the cylinders, which were mounted side by side. Long-skirted pistons of chrome nickel steel worked in 50 x 89mm bores and were joined by a single gudgeon pin, which carried power to the connecting rod. The righthand piston had a flat head, the lefthand piston was domed, to promote turbulence and act as a deflector. Primary induction was via the crankcase and controlled by the righthand piston. The incoming charge passed through a circle of ports and, in filling the chamber, helped to expel spent gases through the exhaust port, still uncovered, in the right cylinder. As the pistons rose together, the charge was compressed and ignited by a single plug on the left; because there was a common combustion chamber, both pistons received the force of the expanding gases.

Another outstanding feature of the first

Garelli was its use of internal-expanding brakes.

Adalberto put his brainchild into the headlines with a winter run through the Moncenisio Pass in northern Italy; further demonstrations, chiefly to show off the engine's low fuel consumption, helped to win him a contract to supply machines to the Italian army.

By 1920 he was searching for more power; he found it following modifications to the fuel supply, which had previously incorporated oil. He put the oil in a separate sump whence it was pumped to a Zenith carburettor with two vaporising chambers, where mixing took place. This meant that, effectively, oil supply was governed by throttle opening. The result was an increase in top speed to 62mph – and increased fuel consumption. Not that this mattered in the world of racing. After initial press

Adalberto in pass-storming gear on a drum-brake Garelli.

Racing Garelli of 1924 with part-megaphone exhaust system.

The 1926 sports version, showing new thinking in exhaust arrangements.

ridicule, Garellis took the first three places in the 350cc class of the 1922 French Grand Prix.

In many of the grands prix of the 1920s the 500 and 350cc classes were run together. For an outright win the 350 Garellis were, naturally, at a disadvantage. However, their light weight, excellent handling and reliability were notable bonus points. Seizing-up was virtually unheard-of; it appeared that the hotter a Garelli became, the better it went. In the Gran Premio delle Nazioni of 1922, held of course at Monza, Guesa took his 350 Garelli through to win ahead of riders mounted on (British) 500s.

Tazio Nuvolari, who went on to become one of the great names in automobile racing, was a Garelli signing for 1923, together with the equally brilliant, though stylistically very different, Achille Varzi.. These two notched up wins for Garelli in five European grands prix and eight Italian events.

But winning does not last for ever. In 1924 Garellis began to disappoint. A win in the 350cc class of the Monza GP was the high point of the year. In 1926 the split-single was seen in the Isle of Man. Erminio Visoli rode one, equipped with four carburettors, in the Junior TT. He had to retire, after a lap during which he worked the single (broken) throttle by wrapping the control cable round a spanner.

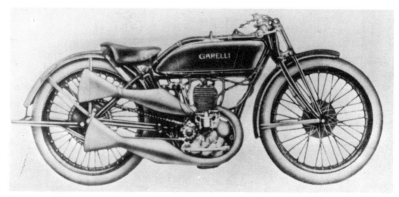

Only one Garelli contested an IoM race. This is the Junior TT entry of 1926.

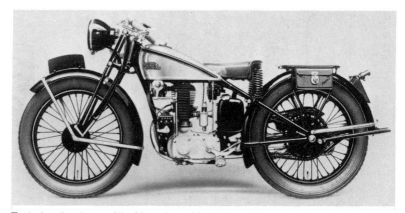

Tested on the slopes of the Matterhorn, this 1934 model was catalogued as the Alpina.

After World War II Garelli reappeared with a motor designed for cycle attachment. It was called the Mosquito, made a suitably mosquito-like noise, and weighed 21lb. It could, said the factory, be fitted to an ordinary pedal cycle in 20 minutes, after which 38cc of two-stroke power was on tap to spin the front wheel via direct roller drive. It became a great commercial success, powering thousands of lazy cyclists at upward...but not much upward...of 20mph. It remained in production throughout the 60s (after acquiring a centrifugal clutch) and formed the basis of all the small two-stroke engines that have been used in successive generations of Garellis.

For long part of the Agrati concern, Garelli have produced a host of 50–75cc lightweights sporting names like Tiger Cross. They have neat cradle frames, pivoted-fork rear suspension, Ceriani – or Ceriani-type – front forks, and a surprising turn of speed.

Garelli Gladiator

In 1956 Italy won the Silver Vase competition in the International Six Days Trial with a team mounted on small four-strokes. Europeans were un-

Stand display at the Milan Show of 1934.

The Mosquito two-stroke, for attachment to bicycles, was manufactured for many years after World War II.

surprised, Americans were astounded; in their eyes rough-riding excellence had long been the prerogative of the screaming two-stroke. In 1969 Garelli exported a few of the 150 Gladiators to the USA, but only a small number of these were sold. *Cycle* magazine's testers were not bowled over. The technical editor looked at the Gladiator and remarked that if the engine were removed, the entire motor cycle would probably collapse into a heap of loose parts.

It was rather ... dismissive; and possibly more indicative of the sketchy nature of the background knowledge of American journalists, who had to refer to the Lola Ford automobile in seeking a parallel for the Gladiator's engine/chassis layout, than the integrity of Garelli's design.

65

Two uprights were bolted to each side of the rear of the engine case, a pair of triangles connecting the forward-top of the case to the steering head. All these members were united by a single straight backbone forming a T, with a connecting point between the uprights. Thus the main load path from the steering head to the rear-fork pivot was through the engine.

The engine/gear unit was canted forward at about 40° from the horizontal, the most noticeable result of this unusual layout being extraordinary clearance from the ground.

The Americans were also, in those days, unused to the sweeping claims of Italy in regard to power, speed and general capability. They viewed Garelli's airy talk of 18bhp and 105mph maximum speed at 8,000rpm with immense (probably justified) reserve and some public distaste. "The Garelli's engine is noticeably old-fashioned," they declared, "with pushrod valve actuation, a 20mm carburettor and a four-speed gearbox. Compression ratio is a modest 9:1, yet claimed power output is two

horsepower per cubic inch. Not bloody likely, for a street-tuned pushrod four-stroke, not even with a claimed cam timing providing 100° of valve overlap. That's race tuning, and the Garelli's power plant just isn't that radical."

Seventy, the critics, said, would be their estimate of true top speed; and no, they were not inclined to put much faith in the tachometer or the speedometer which, they calculated, read fast by a reprehensible 20 per cent.

Specification

Gladiator (1969) *Single-cylinder, ohv, four-stroke. 148cc (58 x 56mm). Four-speed gearbox. 2g fuel. Tyres, 2.75 x 17in (fr), 3.00 x 17in (r). 75mph.*

Gilera

Giuseppe Gilera built his first motor cycle, a 317cc single-cylinder four-stroke with belt final drive, in 1909. Good

A Garelli 70 of the late 50s.

While US riders were adjusting to the strange ways of the Gladiator, this 125 four-stroke, of more conventional appearance, was on sale in Europe.

sales for this, and for the other sv and ohv singles that followed, provided Gilera with the money to move into a factory at Arcore, near Monza. The early years saw continuous growth. In World War I Gilera was the main supplier of motor cycles to the Italian forces, emerging in 1918 as the leading manufacturer.

Gratifying sales of roadsters – mainly 500s – through the 1920s delayed Gilera's entry into sport. In 1930 the firm had a win in the International Six Days Trial centred on Grenoble and repeated it the following year in the Merano-based ISDT. For these and similar sporting events standard ohv 500s modified to single-overhead-camshaft operation were used; by 1932 there were three-valve heads, and chain drive for the ohc had been changed to a train of gears. Internationally, however, the name of Gilera remained obscure, pending arrival of the transverse four that was to take the firm to the pinnacle of racing success in the late 1930s.

The four was not an original Gilera design. It came to Arcore following a mixed career with several other firms. The work of Carlo and Piero Remor, it was developed by Compagnia

Nazionale Aeronautica (CNA) from a basic sohc four-cylinder layout to watercooled, supercharged form, giving 50bhp at 9,000rpm, when it achieved some race successes in 1935 in the hands of Pietro Taruffi.

The following year it was sold to Gilera. By then known as the Rondine (swallow), it had been modified to dohc. Gilera, with Taruffi as contracted rider, made further changes. The crankshaft was strengthened. The front forks became girders, replacing the pressed-steel units previously used. A pivoted fork with horizontally sprung units was fitted at the rear. Under Gilera colours the Rondine was entered for a full race programme following a promising début, in full streamlining and piloted by Taruffi, when it captured an assortment of world speed records. By 1939 it was acknowledged as the fastest motor cycle in the European championship. Dorino Serafini rode one to beat the supercharged BMWs on home ground, in the German GP.

After World War II Gilera had a range of two 500 singles, one a side-valve, the other an overhead-valve, and an ohv 250. The supercharged four was more liability than asset, following the FIM's

Gilera's supercharged, watercooled 500 four of the late 30s – the Rondine.

Running temperature received much attention, with a radiator behind the steering head and a wealth of cooling ribs on the large oil tank. The blower is above the crankcase. Power output of the dohc unit, which drove through a four-speed gearbox, was said to be 92bhp at 8,000rpm.

The Rondine's girder front fork has a central spring and friction dampers. The front brake, like the rear, is a single-side unit with sls operation.

ban on blowers. Gilera's sporting ambitions had to be entrusted to modified versions of the ohv 500 single, the Saturno, while plans were laid to construct a new four.

Like the mid-30s design, this was the work of Piero Remor, who retained the original engine's 52 x 58mm dimensions, but little else. Deep finning and a more upright disposition in the frame obviated any need for water-cooling. Primary and camshaft drives were taken from the middle of the crankshaft, between cylinders two and three. Much light-alloy and a rather skimpy frame helped to keep total weight below 300lb, which was less than that of the rival single-cylinder racers manufactured by Norton. Power was 50bhp, top speed around 125mph. This was too good for the Nortons on any track where the superior handling of the British machines could not be exploited. On a speed bowl such as Monza the four could be relied on to run away from the opposition; at more tortuous tracks the Gilera flag had to be upheld by race-tuned Saturno singles.

It was Geoff Duke's move – popularly

Gilera Saturno 500 single, c1942, restored for use in "classic" meetings of the 80s.

regarded as defection – to Gilera in 1953 that brought the four its near-unbeatable status. Frame and suspension changes were introduced to match the potential of the superb engine (by then producing 60bhp at 10,000rpm). The result was world championship wins in 1953, '54 and '55.

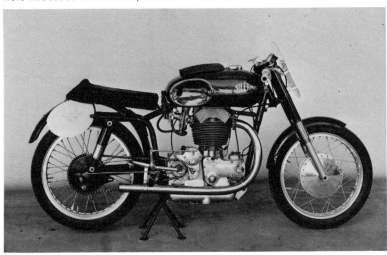

Power of the robust Saturno was increased in the early 50s from under 40bhp to 45bhp at 8,000rpm, while control of the rear pivoted-fork suspension passed from long, high-mounted horizontal springs to conventional, near-vertical units; at the same time the front girders were replaced by telescopics. A favourite with private-owner competitors in national racing, the Saturno could be a match for the better known Manx Norton.

Gilera's unblown four, which made an appearance in 1948. This is a 1949 version. The 30°-inclined dohc engine has paired cylinders, two 28mm carburettors with trumpets and drives a four-speed gearbox from the middle of the crankshaft. The frame, of mixed tubular and pressed construction, carriers torsion-controlled rear suspension.

Other racers turned out by Gilera in the 1950s included 125 and 175cc dohc twins producing in excess of 20bhp, and a 350cc version of the four that drew also on the 175, with a doubling up of the 46 x 52.6mm cylinders of the twin. Gilera road machines were big sellers in the 50s. There was a 125 four-stroke; a 304cc ohv twin, the B300; and a 152cc single. In 1962 Gilera aped Vespa and Lambretta and brought out a scooter, the Chicco. It had a 148cc ohv four-stroke engine and three-speed gearbox mounted on the pivoted arm carrying the rear wheel. It was, like many other imitations of the pioneer postwar scooters, in most respects rather better than the originals but infinitely less successful.

A few years on, after an abortive return to racing under the banner of Scuderia, Duke had been largely forgotten, and with the Japanese stealing export sales, Gilera's star was waning. A takeover by

Private thoughts. From left, Geoff Duke, Piero Taruffi, Commendatore Gilera. With the coming of Duke, in 1953, development of the four quickened. The suspension, already modified to "standard modern" (ie, telescopics, at both ends), was further improved, weight was cut, and internal changes, mainly to valves and combustion chambers, hoisted power to a reputed 65bhp at 10,400rpm.

Top of the world. Geoff Duke on the mid-50s Gilera four, with three consecutive world titles to his credit. Note the advance in brake size, to 250mm diameter, to cope with a top speed on open courses of almost 160mph.

Grey picture faithfully illustrates the appalling conditions of the 1954 Senior TT in the IoM which Duke lost to Ray Amm (Norton) following a controversial early halt in the race.

the Vespa parent company of Piaggio which coveted Gilera's 5,000 sales and service outlets — and, of course, the firm's matchless knowledge of the "pure" motor cycle market — brought financial security to Arcore and an opportunity to plan a fresh assault on the two-wheeler world of the 1970s.

In 1957, during the last year of enveloping "dustbin" fairings, the now-megaphoned four was ridden to great effect by the Scot, Bob McIntyre.

As the manufacturers withdrew from racing at the end of the 1957 season, Gilera signed off with a record-breaking session at Monza in November. This is the "sidecar" outfit used by Albino Milani to cover 116 miles in the hour. He did not, apparently, enjoy the experience.

Gilera's 350 four, first seen at Monza in 1956.

Apart from 125 and 150cc ohv road-going singles (described in some detail in this section), Gilera found openings for a range of sporting 50s which performed to gold-medal standard in the ISDT.

Gilera 175 Standard

First imported into the UK in the summer of 1957, the 175 Gilera continued to be available, though rarely seen, in Britain up to the Piaggio takeover in the late 60s.

Typically "Italian", with much red paintwork of suspect quality, a deep, narrowed-at-the-rear petrol tank, skimpy dualseat, light-alloy wheel rims and exhaust din only a few decibels short of illegality, the 175 shamed British-born bikes of similar capacity. The well-finned engine, with light-alloy head, formed part

The 175 Gilera twin as it appeared in Italian Formula 2 racing in 1957.

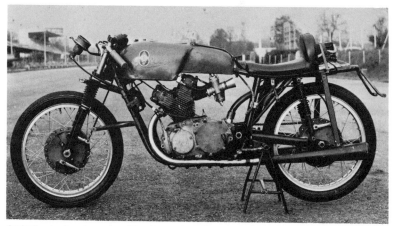

An Italian junior-championship winner, the 175 twin owed much of its design to the all-conquering fours. With cylinder block inclined at 30°, the engine had a central run of gears for dohc valve operation. Bore and stroke were 46 × 52.6mm and top speed, on fifth gear, was 105mph.

of the duplex frame and was, to all practical effect, vibrationless. In addition, it gave plenty of power (9bhp was claimed, at 6,000rpm), and was oil-tight and extremely frugal in fuel-thirst, a figure of 112mpg being returned in one of the constant-speed tests that were a feature of road-test procedure for the motor cycle journals of the day.

Top speed was around 65mph, which was not improved upon when the bike was renamed "175 Sports" in 1958 in an attempt to break through the English market's indifference to imports from the Continent in the years before the Japanese invasion.

Specification

175 Standard (1957) *Single-cylinder, ohv, four-stroke. 172.5cc (60 x 61mm). Four-speed gearbox. 3.5g fuel. Tyres, 2.50 x 19in. 65mph.*

Gilera Arcore 150

Nothing measures up to the authority of firsthand experience. C.E. Allen came late to the joys of small Italian motor cycles, but when he rode a Gilera Arcore he was seduced. He sketches the background to his Italian period...

Lightweight cross-country 50 features a superb frame and long-travel suspension.

A 175 Gilera roadster with Perspex nose treatment.

"Think Gilera and you instantly picture the immortal racing fours, the poetry in motion of Geoff Duke. But the fours, like the rival MVs, were an indulgence of wealthy men who had the backup of extensive sales of bread-and-butter roadster singles, utility two-strokes and mopeds. When Gilera was taken over by Piaggio the range was slimmed to one ohv 125 or 150 and a 50cc two-stroke. The engine of the ohv model was based on the earlier 125–175 range but the machine was completely restyled with a new, welded duplex frame.

"The styling of tank, engine finning and air cleaner, battery box and toolbox section was modern; the new frame was a vast improvement, both in looks and in a practical way, with twin tubes cradling the crankcase, in contrast to the previous arrangement which had them ending at the top of the case. If a really big manufacturer had launched a range

with styling like that, it might have caught on. I had always admired the sporting cafe racer style of the little Gillies in the 50s and 60s, but I did not like this new model, called the Arcore after the factory where it was built...in Germany, I believe, it was called the Strada.

"Not that it mattered to me. In those days an Italian tiddler was just a joke. The Arcore was imported by the Vespa concessionaires. I do not suppose I would ever have given the funny-styled Gilera a second thought had not fate taken a hand and arranged for me to join Douglas Sales as a rep. By this time they had decided the Arcore was a non-starter for volume sales. The intensely loyal Douglas Vespa agents had taken samples into their showrooms and had found them almost impossible to sell against Japanese lightweights. The price was about 25 per cent too high and the 'funny' tank styling did not help.

Arcore 150 of the 70s shows Piaggio's liking for square-cut styling.

Incidentally, the gentle upward slope from the seat was one of the recommendations of an international safety study into motor cycle design. Medical men had told grim tales of crotch injuries caused by racy-looking hump back tanks. Gilera were, to the best of my knowledge, the only makers who adopted the 'safety' tank. I was also told that no Gilera had a propstand because the son of a director had been killed through riding off with a propstand down.

"However, although the dealers who had taken Arcores into stock found them a dead duck as far as sales went, they were impressed with the quality of the bikes. Those few that had been sold had proved to be extremely reliable and long-lasting...so long-lasting, in fact, that the chance of replacement business was nil. In my travels I met the odd owner who swore by his Arcore, not at it, and was wildly enthusiastic. I rode one, of course, and found it a real eye-opener,

having revs aplenty but punch withal, and the super handling and brakes that you only seem to find on Italian bikes.

"I had no use for one at the time, but I kept a look out for one to salt away for the future. A friendly dealer did eventually offer me one, at the right price, and I took it and put it away without even riding it.

"Now that I have time to enjoy a gentle potter round the lanes I am very glad I bought it. It's so light to manhandle, so easy to start once you have mastered the folding lefthand kickstart, and the engine is as eager as a puppy on a leash, always wanting to go faster. The five-speed change is slick, the clutch frees well and grips firmly.

"The steering is light yet completely free from wobble...hands off or one-handed, it is as steady as a rock. The ride is good, with strong forks and firm rear units. And I really do think that it is the first machine I have owned that is overbraked.

Leftside kickstarter may be awkward for an English owner, but the rear-brake pedal, on the same side, is likely to have the approval of older riders. Black canister, at base of the crankcase and adjacent to the brake pedal, is a throwaway oil filter.

"Inevitably one compares it with a CB125 Honda. The performance is about the same but the Gilera has more punch low down, is smoother and quieter mechanically. There is no mechanical noise up to about 50...none of the 'thrash' that puts me off the little Honda. Above 50 there is some indefinable noise which obtrudes, because the exhaust is well muted by the huge silencer. I haven't checked fuel consumption, but it is around 100mpg. It does not use oil, which is just as well because you need a spanner to remove the ridiculously small filler plug at the front of the crankcase and a funnel to pour in the oil. On the other hand, the screw-in oil filter is instantly accessible on the nearside of the crankcase.

"Ignition and lighting is by flywheel magneto, a battery being charged through a rectifier to provide parking lights and flashers. The lights, like those of most Italian models of the period, are simply awful.

"The overall impression is one of real quality, good performance and superlative steering, roadholding and brakes... which is what one would expect from a firm which once led the grand prix scene."

Specification

Arcore 150 (1972) *Single-cylinder, ohv, four-stroke. 152cc (60 × 54mm). Five-speed gearbox. 2.75g fuel. Tyres, 2.75 × 18in (fr), 3.00 × 18in (r). 61mph.*

Gilera B300

At a time (1954) when Gilera could justly claim to build the world's fastest road-racing motor cycle, the decision of this famous concern to turn to what seemed to be the peculiarly English form of the parallel-twin-cylinder was bound to attract attention.

Viewed from the side, a mid-50s B300 was very little different from the earlier 150 single. The engine and crankcase appeared to be no larger; only the greater overall height and deeper fuel tank suggested a capacity change. The explanation was that the 300 was a double-up of the 150, another cylinder being tacked on alongside, on a widened crankcase. It was a straight-forward design, with pushrod operation of overhead valves set in light-alloy cylinder heads, topped by finned lids, for the rocker gear, in the same material. The barrels were of cast-iron. Primary drive was by duplex chain on the left to an in-unit gearbox having four ratios controlled by the right side pedal. Also on this side – a boon to the unhandy English – was the kickstarter.

The frame was of duplex tubing, all welded, carrying a pivoted fork at the rear and front telescopic forks. In early days accommodation was limited to a single, nose-pivoted saddle, replaced in 1957 by the then-usual dualseat. As befitted a company operating in an area of plentiful bauxite, Gilera fabricated many cycle parts in light-alloy, extending this practice even to the large silencer, which was untypically Italian in muffling noise to an astonishing degree. Top speed, too, was unusually subdued: no more than 70mph was possible, rider crouched. More, perhaps, should not have been expected for claimed power was only 12.5bhp at 5,800rpm.

Specification

B300 (1954) *Twin-cylinder, ohv, four-stroke. 304cc (60 x 54mm). Four speed gearbox. 3.6g fuel. Tyres, 3.00 x 18in (fr), 3.25 x 18in (r). 70mph.*

Frigerio-Gilera 230

This was a limited-edition trail – and occasional trials – bike of the early 70s fashioned by the brothers Frigerio, of Treviglio near Bergamo, sons of the Gilera sidecar racer, Ercole, killed in a grand prix crash in 1952. Based on a standard Gilera product, the 230 was finished to a far higher standard than factory machines and was available in Italy at an appropriately inflated price.

The Frigerios fabricated the light-alloy sand-cast cylinder head (incorporating 32mm inlet and 28mm exhaust valves), the widely finned light-alloy barrel, fitted with an austenitic-iron liner, the crank assembly, five-speed in-unit gearbox and toughened clutch. Dual ignition and a 28mm-bore carburettor were featured, and with a compression ratio of 10.2:1

A mid-50s B300 overhead-valve twin.

the engine was said (by the Frigerios) to develop around 21bhp at 7,900rpm. Panels in the rear sub-frame area supported an oil feed for the rear chain (on the right), a comprehensive air-filtration system for the carburettor, and twin coils.

Ceriani-made suspension front and rear gave notably good handling for the 250lb bike, which began its career with a fine showing in the Italian championships against Swedish and Czech two-strokes.

Specification

Frigerio-Gilera 230 (1970) *Single-cylinder, ohv, four-stroke. 230cc (63 x 72mm). Five-speed gearbox. 2.2g fuel. Tyres, 2.75 x 21in (fr), 4.00 x 18in (r).*

Lambretta

Lambretta Model D

Anything that Piaggio did, with their Vespa, was usually followed by a near-identical move on the part of Innocenti, who made the Lambretta. Occasionally the two great scooter innovators acted in concert. Thus in 1954 both concerns exhibited enlarged versions of their trend-setting 125s at the Milan Show. The 148cc Model LD, as the new Lambretta was catalogued, came to Britain in the spring of the following year. In many ways it serves, for these pages, as the archetypal Lambretta.

Always more squat than the Vespa – somehow a little deficient in the *brio* that made its shapely rival so attractive – the Lambretta in the early years of the postwar era seemed, to English eyes, something of a Hurricane fighter plane to the Vespa's Spitfire. Thoroughly decent and reliable, and almost certainly a better handler than the Vespa, because of the more sensibly balanced arrangement of the engine, the LD became extremely popular throughout Europe.

After initial variations, the D series was established with an all-in-one engine-gearbox-transmission unit forming the rear swinging arm, in which movement was controlled by a torsion bar. In earlier, 125, form it was not considered necessary to depress residual surge in the springing system; with an extra 25cc, and the possibility of 40mph speeds, the makers threw in a single hydraulic damper. Lambretta enthusiasts professed to notice a distinct improvement in handling, compared with the 125; strangers to the breed continued to be terrified by the lively ride during their early miles.

The capacity increase was obtained by opening up the 125's bore by 5mm, from 52 to 57mm; the result was an extra 1bhp, on tap lower in the rpm scale than the 125's peak. With a compression ratio of 6.5:1, power rose to 6bhp at 4,750rpm, enough to propel this rather bulky 200lb runabout ... and rider, of course ... at up to 45mph.

Testers employed by the motor cycle journals were wary of the Italian scooters. Hard-riding folk more at home with rumbustious Nortons and the like, they tended to be excused scooter-testing chores, which became the province of the more timid staff members ordinarily engaged in strictly internal matters to do with magazine production. For these quiet men who, with advancing years, had seen their names disappear from "by-line" status, a borrowed Lambretta meant inexpensive commuting for a week or two, with no necessity to look for long-disused all-weather riding gear. Equipped with a screen, a Lambretta was just about guaranteed to keep its rider free of rain, no matter how hard the downpour. As long as he kept going, that is.

This is what *Motor Cycling*'s man had to say on the subject, when he tested a 150 LD ... "The clerk of the weather donated some particularly cutting northerly winds, which served to show that the weather protection provided by the combination of footboards, shield and screen was as complete as that of an open motor car. It was quite possible to ride the Lambretta when dressed in normal office-going rig and with no more hand protection than a pair of woollen gloves. There was little or no evidence of cavitation behind the shield, and it is certain that even quite heavy rain would not have resulted in a spot of moisture reaching the rider's garments." (Assurance in the matter of no evident cavitation must have influenced many a potential buyer.)

Twistgrip-controlled gears (three) had well-judged ratios to make the most of the Lambretta's useful power spread, with the result that acceleration was as good as that of the majority of British-made lightweight motor cycles of similar capacity.

Specification

LD 150 (1955) *Single-cylinder, two-stroke. 148cc (57 x 58mm). Three-speed gearbox. 1.5g fuel. Tyres, 4.00 x 8in. 44mph.*

Lambretta/Bambini

Not so mindless a proposition as a dedicated motor cyclist might have imagined, a low-powered scooter/sidecar outfit had charms all its own (among which, perhaps needless to say, performance in any noticeable way did not figure).

In the mid-50s Watsonian, the well-known English sidecar manufacturer, was persuaded to turn out a model specifically for fitting to the Italian scooters that were contributing so forcefully to the decline of the native motor cycle industry. The Bambini, as it was called, was a one-piece moulding in glass-fibre; attachment was by a single-tube chassis running to a resilient coupling on a clamp fitted to the scooter's main frame member. The sidecar's tiny wheel (at 8in a match for the typical scooter's) was held in pivoted-arm suspension.

A scooter "combo" in, say, 1956 might have been a 148cc Lambretta/Bambini. The sidecar makers – Watsonian was the chief one, but there were others – had waited until Lambretta had a 25cc boost before dragging out the drawing board. Nobody rated the bigger Lambretta a dazzling performer, but the capacity increase had bestowed extra torque where it was most needed, with sidecar hauling in mind.

Cruising speed was 30–35mph, with 40mph available on downgrades. There was much call on second gear when winds were unfavourable or the going was hilly. Lambrettas could be obtained with special "sidecar" gearing.

As might be expected, with rubbery suspension all round, a trailing-link front fork, and miniature wheels, steering was not of the "hair-line" variety. It was not advisable to remove hands – or even one hand – from the handlebar; doing so usually resulted in a flutter that could worsen into a full-scale wobble. As for the Bambini, it was prettily styled and reasonably comfortable for a moderate-size adult; anybody measuring over 5ft 7in tended to loom at eye-watering height above the tiny screen. There was no door and, many things considered, the Bambini was best reserved for the more supple members of a scooterist's family circle. As *The Motor Cycle* put it, in inimitable style: "Entry and exit called for a slight measure of physical dexterity."

Specification

Lambretta/Bambini (1956) *Single-cylinder, two-stroke. 148cc (57 x 58mm). Three-speed gearbox. 1.4g fuel. Tyres, 4.00 x 8in; sidecar, 3.50 x 8in 34mph.*

Laverda

Laverda's founder, Pietro Laverda, had nothing to do with motor cycles. He set up a factory in Breganza in 1873 to make farm machinery. It was his grandson, Francisco, who first put the family name to a motor cycle. This was in 1949 when Italy was starved of cheap transport. There was little demand for fast, expensive two-wheelers. Workers wanted runabouts that would keep going for a week on a gallon of *benzina*; the scooter makers had realised this early on. Francisco's motor cycle had a 74cc (45 x 46mm) four-stroke engine with overhead valves operated by pushrods. The construction was all-alloy, the barrel having an iron liner, and power output was 3bhp at 5,200rpm. The pressed-

steel frame was in the form of a sloping spine carrying simple, pressed forks and an egg-shaped fuel tank at the front, with the inclined-cylinder engine/gear unit underneath, and pivoted-fork rear suspension. The gearbox had three speeds with rocking-pedal control on the right. It was almost elegant, with 17/18in wheels, and there were one or two little touches of Laverda individuality: pillion footrests, for example, that could be unbolted and used as tyre levers.

With a top speed between 40 and 45mph, it proved to be extremely reliable (and, as the years passed, durable). Five hundred or thereabouts were made in 1951, a year in which some interest in racing was evinced when a simple form of friction damping, adjustable by hand, was introduced at the rear, and a team of four was entered for the 700-mile Milan–Taranto run. Rather to the surprise of Francisco and his workers, all four finished. The 75 was developed, with a high-compression piston, race-type camshaft, larger carburettor, and a special head; the result, according to Laverdas, was 10bhp at 13,000rpm. There may be some doubt regarding the accuracy of this figure ... 130bhp/litre, in 1953, may raise an Anglo-Saxon eyebrow ... but there is no denying the hotted-up 75's impressive race record, which extended to class wins in the Milano–Taranto event of 1953, and the same year's Giro d'Italia.

Bored and stroked (to 52 x 47mm), the 75 became a 100 for 1954 and was installed in a new tubular frame with telescopic forks and more conventional-looking rear suspension, with twin spring units. The 75, too, appeared with the tubular frame. Both engine sizes, available in Turismo and Sport forms, were the basis of Laverda's range through most of the 1950s, bringing in a substantial revenue that funded, in 1960, one of designer Luciano Zen's long-pondered projects. He had determined to tap the market exploited to great effect by Lambretta and Vespa. The Laverda scooter, when it appeared, was a light, pretty device that graduated from 50cc and two speeds to 60cc and a three-speed gearbox within a year. With a top speed of no more than 30mph, but

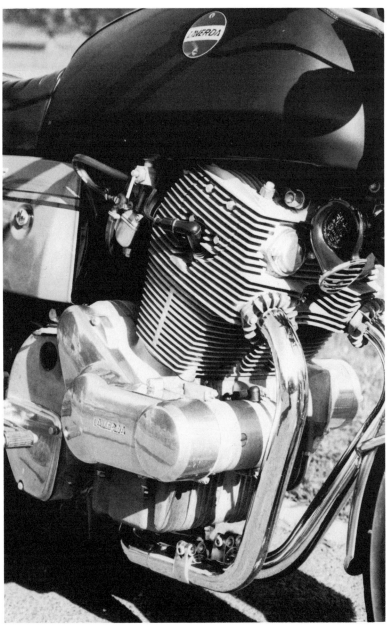

Big twin that "bore much superficial resemblance to the Honda CB 72/77 series".

offering outstanding economy, at around 180mpg, the scooter continued to be sold up to 1962, when the 200 twin-cylinder Laverda was introduced.

This had bore and stroke measurements of 52 x 47mm and oh valves operated by pushrods, and in many other ways followed the design of the 100 single. A pressed-steel spine was incorporated into a basically tubular frame. Full-width hubs (designed for the last of the 100s) carried two leading-shoe brakes. The engine was mounted in rubber and developed 11bhp at 6,500rpm; top speed was around 70mph. It had a long production run of eight years, to 1968, and a year or two into its life was taken up by the affluent among American motor cyclists who craved something more interesting than the Japanese lightweights. It was sold in the USA under the aegis of the Garelli organisation. In 1965 a new Laverda with horizontal 125cc single-cylinder appeared. Beautifully engineered, with top-class Ceriani forks and a wealth of

other expensive proprietory items, it was sold in the US alongside the 200 where it came to the attention of importer Jack McCormack, then a Honda con-cessionaire in America.

When he started his "own brand" concern in 1968 it was to Laverda that he turned for a Honda-style twin to sell under the American Eagle title. Thus Laverda's first big twin, introduced as a 650 in 1966 but within a few months enlarged to 750cc, bore much superficial resemblance to the Honda CB72/77 series. The 750 twin began life as a mild-mannered tourer, under a GT label, but was soon developed to S and SF form; the final variation was the SFC, a roadgoing production racer that is presently much sought-after by Laverda enthusiasts.

In 1970, as an S, with Laverda's own brakes replacing the original Grimecas, the 750 won three events, to give the factory a foundation for its enviable record in 750cc-class production racing. Though these winning machines – and

The 500 Alpino photographed on a coast road in Portugal.

Short-lived derivative of the Alpino was a similarly styled 350 twin.

In the mid-70s Laverda retained an interest in small motor cycles, turning out a succession of well-styled lightweights powered, for the most part, by units bought in from abroad. Thus this 175, together with a similar 125, was fitted with a watercooled Zündapp single. Having the impeccable road manners expected of a Laverda, and surprising power, for their capacity, they should have been popular. In fact, overshadowed by the bigger machines in the range, they proved to be indifferent sellers.

more particularly the following year's SFC series – bore more than a few marks of the tuner's craft, the engine, even in standard form, was from the outset a rare performer.

The one-litre three-cylinder first appeared at the Milan Show of 1969 but was not offered for sale until 1973. Its large camboxes militated against the use of the twin's spine-type frame. A semi-cradle type was settled on, with a 2½in-diameter main member bearing most weight, with triangulation around the steering head. With its narrow crankshaft, low-slung engine and lightweight frame, the triple, released as the 3C, was within 10lb or so of the 750, developed more power, and handled, if not impeccably, at least predictably, and in the manner expected of an 80bhp, 130mph Italian "thoroughbred".

The 500cc Alpino, with dohc and four-valve heads, and later developed as the more sporting Montjuic, never achieved the standing of the larger Laverdas. Undeniable individuality and fine build quality (let down on occasion by the paint finish) have never altogether outweighed the facts of high price and relatively "so-so" performance.

Another Laverda with small-capacity engine was this 125 would-be moto-crosser (with headlamp) powered by a two-stroke single supplied by Husqvarna of Sweden.

Laverda Sports 75

The patronising attitude of the 1950s English motor cycling press to stylish Italian motor cycles of less than 100cc is well illustrated by the following: "It is really surprising that so few British riders evince interest in the fascinating under-100cc class. There is joy in handling a really good 'ultra-light', and it requires far greater driving skill to use the available power to the best advantage. By comparison, the user of a 500 is a mere lorry-driver...".

The truth of the matter is that British-made "ultra-lights" of the time were so feeble that they deserved to arouse little interest. All the riding skill in the world would have been wasted in any attempt to turn their scanty "available power" to a respectable end. The same could not be said of continental machines, which in many cases were startlingly powerful for their capacity; but, then, few of these were imported into the UK.

A 75cc Sports Laverda of 1954 was a case in point. With a swept volume almost precisely 50 per cent of that of the D3 BSA Bantam, it managed to be both faster and more economical, and was incomparably more pleasing to the eye.

There were three versions of this overhead-valve Laverda: touring, sports and MT (for Milano–Taranto). (Why, one asks, didn't BSA ever christen one of their bikes BL, for Birmingham–London? Midlands folk – Midlands motor cycle-manufacturing folk, especially – are so fiercely parochial, so devoted to the idea of Birmingham as the hub of the universe, that the only initials they might approve of in this context would be BB ... which, come to think of it, was how one of the Gold Star series was listed.)

The Laverda's engine was "oversquare", at 46 x 45mm, with both barrel and head in light-alloy. A flywheel generator supplied current to an external coil, with a contact-breaker mounted on the left side of the camshaft. Oil was carried in a 2pt-capacity reservoir integral with the crankcase, which also incorporated the gearbox. At the rear was a long-travel pivoted fork with twin dampers; at the front, a telescopic fork.

Power outputs ranged from 3.7bhp at 6,500rpm for the touring model, sufficient for a maximum speed of 40mph, to 4.7bhp/7,500rpm for the Sports (55mph), to 5.5bhp/8,600 for the MT, which was credited with 60mph. Fuel consumption averaged 140mpg for all these models, only one of which, the MT, was equipped with a four-speed gearbox, in place of the normal three-speeder.

Only one test report has been studied, It relates to the 150lb sports version, which had an 8:1 compression ratio and 16mm-choke carburettor. A maximum speed of 55mph was obtained with the rider crouched low over the tank; when he was sitting up, speed dropped by about 4mph. The brakes performed excellently, bringing the bike to a halt in 30ft from 30mph, the standard so long aimed for by English manufacturers.

In typical Italian fashion, the tiny Laverda could be ridden flat out on the autostrada for miles on end ... more in lorry-driver style than as an exercise of great driving skill, to the compiler's mind.

Specification

Sports 75 (1954) *Single-cylinder, ohv, four-stroke. 74.75cc (46 x 45mm). Three-speed gearbox. 1.8g fuel. Tyres, 2.375 x 20in. 55mph.*

Laverda SF750

In 1973 Laverda were making four models – three 750 twins and a three-cylinder 1000. A year earlier the compiler had ridden an SF750 to Cologne in company with BMF official Bruce Preston who, possibly for patriotic reasons, and if so, misguidedly, elected to ride a well-used 750 twin from the Norton factory. The Laverda never, as they say, missed a beat and turned out to be much more than a high-revving sportster by unconcernedly towing the sickly Commando through much of Belgium. Both riders returned to the UK with a high opinion of the Laverda.

Quite a few changes were made to the SF for '73, as Preston found out when he borrowed an example for a couple of weeks.

It was, of course, a twin-cylinder

four-stroke with duplex chain drive to a single overhead camshaft. The chain was sensibly retained by a split link so that it was not necessary to remove the crankshaft if there was a need to replace the chain(!). One of the new developments for 1973 was a cylinder head developed from that employed in the production racer SFC version. It came as a package designed to make the machine "effortlessly faster". Larger, 36mm, carburettors incorporated a mechanical, car-type injection-pump for starting. Blipping the throttle resulted in

a squirt of petrol in the right place – and, if overdone, a "wet" plug. There was a new air cleaner, of paper-element type. Compression ratio had taken a drop, from 9.5:1 to 8.9:1, enabling 3-star petrol to be used. Another significant change was a redesign of the exhaust system to comply with strict German silencing laws. It's true that the previous arrangement was a bit *sporting*: the new pipes had a large-diameter connector tube and were, uncharacteristically for this looks-conscious firm, a little on the ugly side.

The 750SF rider is not disregarding the white line. The setting is France. In the background is the parked Commando of the photographer. Note the 11in front drum brake of this 1972 model.

Returning to the engine layout (and the present tense) ... the camshaft-actuating chain runs between the cylinders, and the shaft has four bearings. The crankshaft, too, has four bearings, two spanning the double camshaft sprocket inside the flywheel, and one at each end. Outside the righthand main bearing is a sprocket for chain drive to the starter motor, a 1hp

Early 750SF Laverdas were offered with a choice of single- or dual-seat.

A police model, retaining Laverda's own drum brakes.

device mounted behind the engine and above the gearbox. At the righthand end of the crankshaft is a pulley for the belt to the forward-mounted 150w dynamo. The lefthand end is a mite crowded, too, with, first, a treble sprocket to take the triplex primary chain, then a smaller gear, sharing the same drive spline and running to the oil pump drive gear, reputed to give a turn-round of three litres of lubricant a minute. The contact-breaker assembly is mounted outboard of the oil gear. All in all, these components make for a rather wide engine – and a good case for fitting crash bars.

The crankcase splits horizontally to reveal the internals of the five-speed gearbox and the crankshaft. The seven-plate clutch is housed at the left side. (At this time Laverda fitted the gearchange on the right – the "traditional" British side; soon after, it was taken over to the left, to suit America and other profitable markets.)

The electrics, although predominantly Bosch, were not German throughout, for the headlamp was a Laverda design, though very BMW-like, and many of the controls were manufactured by Lucas, with English waywardness on show in wiring of the flashing indicators to give "up" for right and "down" for left, opposing the general fashion. The magnificently raucous horn was made by Fiamm of Italy, the speedometer and tachometer came from a Japanese company (succeeding Smiths Industries).

The frame. How to describe it? Using the engine as part of the chassis, the frame consisted of two robust top tubes running from the head to the rear of the dualseat. A further pair of tubes looped up from the rear swing-arm pivot, meeting the two top tubes for about 12in and then curving down to join the bottom

Interim stage: single front disc brake, wire-spoke wheels, and collector box linking the exhaust pipes.

of the steering head. A tendency to roll, noted in the "Cologne" model, had been eliminated. Front and rear suspension units were made by Ceriani, and the brakes were Laverda's own, beautifully made, each of 230mm diameter and having 21s operation. They were outstanding, Preston found, and went on..."We were not too happy with the choice of seat on a previous Laverda, because it was a single unit, and, well, there are occasions when company is appreciated. What we didn't realize was that there was an option of racing seat or dualseat. Many buyers take both, apparently. This test bike had a dualseat. In most respects it was very good, but it conspired with two of the machine's other virtues to create something of a problem. It sloped forward, and the fuel tank was quite deep at the rear. When a pillion passenger was carried, and the brakes were used with any firmness, the passenger would vacate the rear part of the seat, thrusting the unwary pilot painfully into the tank. Still, a minor quibble."

"Just to sit astride the SF was a pleasure," wrote Preston. "It felt about as good as a motor cycle can feel. If one had to form an opinion without riding anywhere, it would be that this has to be one of the best motorcycles." In the main, he didn't change his views when he did ride somewhere, though vibration ... not so much vibration as a sort of heavy throbbing ... intruded a little. He liked the instant starting... "A brief stab at the button and the engine boomed to life, a Robeson, throaty sound. They say the silencers have been redesigned, and it is true the bike is quieter than last year's model; but by no stretch of the imagination may it be termed *quiet.*"

The Laverda's tickover was at a steady 600/700rpm, with mechanical noise being very subdued.

Finally, throwing patriotism to the winds, Preston opined that the Laverda was "really too good for this country. It is, supremely, a high-speed tourer, able to cruise for hundreds of miles at very high speed, looking as cool, calm and collected at the end of a run as at the start."

He was probably right, for the SF, long discontinued, has collectable status these days.

Specification

SF750 (1973) *Twin-cylinder, ohc, four-stroke. 748cc (79.5 x 76mm). Five-speed gearbox. 4g fuel. Tyres. 3.50 x 18in (fr), 4.00 x 18in (r). 117mph.*

Laverda Montjuic

Never a wild success in the UK, the Montjuic was a beautifully engineered replica racer that was too uncompromising in its devotion to performance at any price to appeal to members of the "café-racer" brigade who had been softened up by experience of less expensive offerings from the Japanese manufacturers. Their loss, of course; for the Montjuic was a classic of its kind.

Based on the more civilized but lack-lustre Alpino model, the Montjuic had dohc, an eight-valve head and a pedigree that included wins in Barcelona 24-hour races. The idea for it – a "street-legal" racer – originated in the fertile brain of Roger Slater, for long the

This later SF, with cast-alloy wheels and twin disc brakes, has been fitted with a non-standard exhaust system.

English importer of Laverdas. In 1981 (which Laverda said would be the final year for production of the 500 twin) the Montjuic as sold in Britain was equipped with a half-fairing and streamlined seat pan made by Screen and Plastic.

The engine developed 52bhp at 9,000rpm, with the co-operation of a black- (soon rust-) finished megaphone exhaust system that guaranteed public awarness of a Montjuic's passing. Reasoning that a Montjuic's owner, whether track-orientated or not, would be young, supple and unwilling to let another vehicle pass him, the makers omitted rear-view mirrors and turn signals. Dropped bars, high-mounted footrests (in forged alloy), downdraught 36mm Dellortos unencumbered by air-cleaners, and Japanese-made speed dials were distinguishing features. The wheels were five-spoke, of cast aluminium, to Laverda design; the brake discs were rust-prone but effective 10in-diameter Brembos, two at the front, one at the rear; the suspension, both ends, was by Marzocchi.

With admirably close ratios for the six-speed gearbox, reassuring handling, fine brakes and powerful, vibratory engine, the Montjuic impressed as a fine, if somewhat antisocial, tool for rapid riding on A roads. On the track, and contrary to what its endurance exploits might have suggested, it failed to make much impression on oriental opposition.

But ... a collector's piece (even at £2,400).

Specification

Montjuic (1981) *Twin-cylinder, dohc, four-stroke. 497cc (72 x 61mm). Six-speed gearbox. 3.1g fuel. Tyres, 100/90 x 18in (fr), 110/90 x 18in (r). 115mph.*

The 500 Montjuic enjoyed a brief vogue in formula racing.

Laverda V6

Journalists at the Laverda factory in Breganza in 1977 sneaked tantalising glimpses of a rare machine which culminated (after a little pressure had been applied to the brothers Laverda) in a memorably ear-tingling audience during which some of the finer points of this potential flagship of the range were revealed.

The bike was not, even at this stage, completely strange to the visiting scribes. The existence of a V6 had been an open secret for more than a year, but very few other than highly placed factory personnel had seen the machine. The intention was that it should head the Laverda line-up, spawning smaller modular derivatives with fewer cylinders to establish in time a completely new range to take the place of existing 500 and 750 twins (the latter already being withdrawn) and 1000 triples.

Nothing came of the plan, for reasons which remain obscure, as far as direct information from the factory is concerned, but may be judged as having much to do – surprise, surprise – with ever-steepening costs. Piero, one of the Laverda brothers, said: "The modern trend is to less complicated engines, and this is what we are looking at now."

Four V6 engines were built, and two chassis. A complete machine was shown at the 1977 Milan show; another (or, possibly, the same one) was raced at the Bol d'Or at Paul Ricard in 1978. It retired early after impressing as having plenty of speed and a fine exhaust note. There was trouble with the transmission. It was the last "official" appearance of the V6 Laverda.

Twin-bank six, set at a 90° vee, has four-valve heads.

Handsome V6 racer appeared in 1977.

The V6 was designed by a small team headed by Laverda's then technical director, Luciano Zen, with consultative assistance from Giulio Afieri, famed in automotive circles for his work on, among other engines, the Maserati 3-litre V6. The twin banks of three watercooled cylinders, each with chain-driven dohc, were set at 90° to each other, with 120° phasing of the cranks, and four valves to each head. Oil was carried in an under-seat tank, which supplied a dry-sump system. Ignition was by Marelli – and was probably electronic – and carburation by six vertical Dellortos. Fuel injection was considered, and might have been installed had the project matured. The five-speed gearbox was connected to a shaft final drive. The Marzocchi front forks were conventional, as was the frame; rear suspension was to be either by horizontal monoshock or two inclined spring units working on an ordinary pivoted fork.

The V6's brief outing at Paul Ricard supported rumours emanating from the factory that suggested over 130bhp and 170mph(!) for the machine in racing form.

Specification

V6 (1977) *Six-cylinder, dohc, four-stroke. 995.5cc (65 x 50mm). Five-speed gearbox. 6g fuel. Tyres, 4.00 x 18in (fr), 5.00 x 18in (r).*

Laverda 1200

Laverda, valuing the North American market, modified the 1000 triple in a number of ways in 1978 and sent the result to the USA in the fervent hope that it would erase, or at least assuage, the impression created by the earlier Jota. The 981cc version had not, it appeared, gone down very well. It had been too obviously a racer detuned only a trifle for use on those 55mph-governed

1200 variations. This one has subdued styling and raised handlebar.

highways; that, at any rate, was how the Americans saw it – as a bike prepared for "hard-core" sport. On the legislative front, restrictions were impending that would limit the Jota's life, for its gearshift location and exhaust emission standards were keyed to European usage.

Basically, the 1000 was changed to meet what the Laverda family imagined the wealthy American motor cyclist was looking for in his imported toy. The bore was increased by 5mm, to give 1115cc (the 1200 title being bestowed on a rounding-up principle), and compression ratio reduced from 10:1 to 8:1; the carburettors, 32mm Dellortos, remained unchanged, as did the camshaft form. The intention was clear. Laverda were after approximately the same power put out by the earlier 1000 but in a softer, more manageable form. Further, they were looking for greater torque, lower in the rev-band, to cope with higher gearing.

As one commentator declared: "The 1200 is stronger and less efficient and quieter and there's less of a surge as the engine comes into its optimum rev-band, although because there is so much power from either version, that is not something one notices."

The engine was phased at 180°, following the pattern of the original triple.

Suspension had been softened a little, compared with the 1000, with less rebound damping in the front forks. Tipping the rear spring units forward effectively reduced their spring rate; both compression and rebound damping had been increased, but the new location for the top mounts largely cancelled the effects of the changes. Steering angle was increased from 26.5° to 28°, the consequent gain in trail being balanced by moving the fork legs nearer to the steering head; all with the objective of retaining good straightline steering while reducing the labour involved in slow-speed turns.

The 1200 Mirage fitted with bikini fairing and matching screen. Note new-for-1980 drilled discs.

The once-adjustable handlebar had been mounted higher, the fuel tank capacity increased a trifle, and the rear-chain size set at no. 630 ("about the size you'd pick for towing aircraft out of the harbour", said *Cycle World*).

Criticism of Laverda was not silenced in the USA by this new purpose-built bolide. The seat, on a motor cycle purporting to be something of a grand tourer, was not kindly received. It was criticised as being more seat pan than seat; and its narrowness too, was unpopular. Then there was the clutch, which was so heavy that it was sending 1200 owners off to gyms in search of muscle power. And the side-stand, which was spring-loaded for self-return and angled to hold $4,200-worth of motor cycle only a degree or two before instant topple. And the oil-filler neck which, according to the acerbic reviewer quoted earlier, was "cunningly

calculated to ensure some spillage during toppings-up, even if you've got a hand like some hotshot surgeon from M*A*S*H".

Was the 1200 the breakthrough that Laverda were looking for in America? Probably not....

Specification

1200 (1978) *Three-cylinder, ohc, four-stroke. 1,115cc (80x 74mm). Five-speed gearbox. 4.8g fuel. Tyres, 4.20 x 18in (fr), 4.25 x 18in (r). 124mph.*

Laverda Jota 120

Laverdas, the big ones especially, might be said to be ideally suited to the More Mature Motor Cyclist.

If (in the UK) it is accepted that the majority of motor cyclists are aged 17 to 25, this means that in the 1980s they have been raised, in the main, on

Early 3C 1000 triple with wire wheels.

Japanese products, and thus have become accustomed to utterly civilised transport. They will be used to efficient braking, instant starting, comfort, faultless electrics, a light clutch, an abundance of smooth, manageable power, an inoffensive exhaust.

Only 10 years back the situation was rather different. The *British* motor cycle was much more recent history then. As it disappeared, young motor cyclists hooked on the British style tended to switch to Italian imports, which served up something of the same spare, muscular power. Now aged around 30 years old, earning probably more than the average take-home pay packet, this hypothetical enthusiast is an ideal candidate for Jota ownership. He, and anybody else who sees a motor cycle as an instrument for pure personal enjoyment that is utterly absorbing ... almost certainly utterly selfish ... anti-social (if by anti-social is meant disregarding the well-being of old ladies' ear drums) ... and is destined to bring him sooner or later to a magistrates' court, because of basic incompatibility between the Jota way of life and speed-limit observance. In short, this is a very disturbing, and desirable machine. Were the second Flood to come in the 1980s, and twentieth-century Noah have the good sense to stipulate one motor cycle for the inventory, it might as well be a Jota.

A 120 Jota, of course. The "traditional" Jota triple was – is – of 180 layout, with the two outer pistons moving in unison a stroke away from the opposing middle piston. Though no drawback as a power-producer, this arrangement gives rise to vibration severe enough to debilitate a rider on a long run. There can be little doubt that the Jota's reputation, and sales, suffered from stories which made more of the *stamina* required in riding far and fast on a 180 triple than of the power available. With the arrival of the 120 there was a resurgence of enthusiasm for this superbly crafted motor cycle.

Outwardly, there is little to distinguish a 120 from a 1981 (180) model. The main change is internal, to the crankshaft, which has been rejigged for optimum primary balance, with the cranks staggered at equal intervals on 360°, with attendant modifications to cams and timing. A Jota buff, of course, would notice in seconds that there are rubber mounts for the engine (most obviously, at one point in front and two at the rear, though we gather that there are in all six attachments), where before it was a simple matter of nuts and bolts; that the clutch is hydraulically operated; that the gear change/foot brake arrangements follow the Japanese pattern.

The Jota offers a superb riding position for the open road; in town it directs too much weight on the arms. The rider's knees are in gentle contact with the curve of the feed pipes for the triple Dellortos. The rearswept bar, angled to suit the fairing and dropping by just the right amount, measures no more than 24 inches. The seat, seemingly a little lower than on 180 Jotas, at 32in, is short, narrow and surprisingly comfortable for upward of three hours. The footrests are high and far back, in close company with gear and brake pedals, both of which are mounted on splines providing adjustment.

Starting is pretty well instantaneous at a prod of the button, provided that the choke lever, conveniently mounted on the clutch-lever fulcrum, is in use. A few revolutions for warm-up, and the choke may be pushed back; to be required, just as briefly, if subsequently the engine is allowed to cool for more than a few minutes.

When the engine fires, the man on the bike will be aware of the fact. Not, as in the past, with the 180 engines, because of vibration at bar, footrests and other extremities and an exhaust crackle that would be acceptable at Monza autodrome; no, on the 120 it's mainly the exhaust din that is the clue to life below. The silencers on this latest Jota are no longer the Contis favoured in years past. These days they are made in the UK by Healeys, who have eschewed original design work to follow instead the lead of the Italian makers, by ensuring as little obstruction as possible for gases, and phons. The result is delightful ... well, *almost* delightful.

Views in the matter must be subjective. In conscience, we have to say that when returning home to a sleeping suburb at 10 pm (well, that's the way it is in north London, in the Thatcher years), circumnavigating the old people's homes that proliferate in a caring community, a twinge of doubt occasionally marred enjoyment of the deep chest tones of this uninhibited roadburner. More to the point, it was possible to detect, during even the most pussyfooting excursion, a sudden extra alertness in the demeanour of any policeman in exhaust-note range. The result was rider-unease. Nothing extreme, you understand: more a reluctance to hang about in traffic alongside Panda cars or to risk any situation that might throw up a confrontation with any veteran law-enforcer weaned on LE Velo decibels.

The clutch is hydraulically operated, as mentioned earlier; in total there are three fluid reservoirs dotted about on handlebar and rear frame, to take care of the clutch and the three 11in-diameter Brembos. All have old-fashioned screw-down tops, instead of the bolt-down type favoured by the security-conscious Japanese manufacturers. We have been told, by Jota men, that the Laverda clutch, in the old days devoid of hydraulic assistance, used to tax the strongest hand; by comparison, these experts say, the 120's is featherlight. Perhaps; but we note that enthusiast Tim Parker continues to advise the dedicated Jota rider to flex a tennis ball in his left hand ... presumably when he is off the machine ... in order to build up muscle tone. This, of course, is merely one example of the mystique that goes with ownership of any out-of-the-ordinary vehicle such as a Jota. It would not have been a total surprise to find Parker advocating a course in karate: "Master the neck-grip and you'll never have to worry about front-end weave."

Unlike some Japanese contemporaries, the Jota does not develop upwards of 100 horses. The rumoured

In early 1979 some 3CL models, by then on cast-alloy wheels and sporting an oil cooler, were named Jarama and reduced in price, for the UK market, to a pound or two under £2,000. A choice of left- or right-side gear change was provided.

figure is 85. However, as these are lusty Italian *cavalli* they are numerous enough to propel this 550lb bike to 140mph, or thereabouts, in the hands of testers with access to timing-strip facilities – and to 130, or thereabouts, with the writer aboard, and on some rather less official occasion, at which point the rpm needle was entering the 7,500 red-line area.

Cruising speed depends more – much more – on rider and situation than on the Jota. Given the right environment, which appears these days to have dwindled to some sections of the German autobahn system, there is no reason to believe that the Jota, and the right sort of rider, sheltered by the aerodynamic fairing, would object to a sustained 120-125mph. In a land such as ours, where high speed is often dangerous, and always illegal, it was noted time and again that it was very inviting, on reasonable A or B roads, to settle to a rhythm which impressed the rider, without recourse to the speedometer, as being 70-ish – but turned out to be around 140kph (the instrument on our machine being thus calibrated), or 85-and-a-bit.

The ABS fairing is smoothly finished, ribbed in fibreweave and aluminium strip, and carried on very robust supports. It did a good job of keeping wind and rain off most of the rider's upper body, contributing to an easy, untired passage. Its only drawback was that, shrouding the handlebar quite closely, it prevented use of rear-view mirrors. A bar-end mirror might have been possible, or one of those tiny, rather ineffective devices that clip on to the screen.

In a society obsessed with facts and figures, it might be useful to quantify the incidence of licence endorsements per 100 miles of Jota usage, preferably with similar data on other high-powered motor cycles. An eccentric project, admittedly, but were it to be undertaken we believe that the Jota would head the list. This would reflect (a) its speed, (b) the average owner's reluctance to hang about at tickover speeds in top gear (70mph = 4,100rpm), and (c) the little matter of no rear-view mirrors. Possibly less supple than the ideal Jota man, and

It requires a trained Laverda observer to tell a "120" Jota from the earlier version. *Above* – the "180" model; *below* – the later, smoother-running "120".

more dependent on a mirror, we found that rearward flicks of the head, while riding in a semi-crouch, were of little help. Massed battalions of constabulary might have timed our progress, and we should have been unaware of them. Riding this mirrorless Jota produced a kind of fatalism. Loath though we were to see the bike returned to the concessionaires there was a knife-edge quality about our time with it, as if it were going to be a close-run thing between handing it back and collecting a ticket.

Handling was of near-racer, or Ducati Pantah, standard, The brakes? There are none better, though possibly the rear one was a little sharp, with any wheel-locking tendency exaggerated by weight transfer during use of the immensely powerful front discs.

We used the flyback side stand for a while, though its absurd geometry put the Jota at risk when parked on other than a carefully selected surface. On the third night of the test we had the good sense, or luck, to use the centre stand ... no hardship, in fact, because the bike rolls back and up with very little effort. The following morning it was convenient to use the side stand for a minute or two, before moving off. When a tall, weighty object such as a 981cc Laverda, with a large red tank, begins slowly, oh so slowly, to keel over, the effect is slightly unreal. An immediate reaction is, idiotically, to question the equilibrium of the pavement. Has surburbia been chosen for the Apocalypse? What's new on the Richter scale? Then "it's those balancer canals – what are they called? – in the ears. Another second and you're going to fall over and be very sick." And finally, of course, your eyes drop to the side stand and it is clear that this miserable device is buckling, millimetre by millimetre. When this incident was recounted to Tim Parker, the Laverda expert, he said, a little tersely: "I can see you haven't studied my book on Laverdas. I recommend that Triple owners should throw the side stand away without delay."

Nothing else loosened, bent or self-destructed. The engine would settle to an overslow tickover that was not fully reliable, but this was not unexpected, with an engine to Jota tune. Getting into neutral at a standstill could be a hit-or-miss business. No other criticisms are worth airing. Fuel consumption cannot be counted a disappointment, for it varied between 40 and 32mpg, with a range of almost 150 miles available, on average, from fill-up to switching on the reserve supply.

In the pure spirit of inquiry, the writer tested reserve to the penultimate drop (true), and confirms that any Jota owner reduced to reserve during a bank holiday spin in the Outer Hebrides has approximately 31 miles left to him before he has seriously to consider his next move....

Specification

Jota 120 (1982) *Three-cylinder, ohc, four-stroke. 981cc (75 x 74mm). Five-speed gearbox. 4.3g fuel. Tyres, 100/90V x 18in (fr), 120/90V x 18in (r). 138mph.*

A rung or two down from Laverda's top model . . . the RGA 1000.

Laverda RGA

New in 1983, the RGA was built to satisfy a request from Laverda's UK importers for a cheaper version of the RGS. The main difference was a small headlamp fairing, in place of the half-fairing of the RGS. Some hundreds of pounds less expensive than the top-of-the-range models, the RGA was touted as a fine example of how to maximise the sales potential of the three-cylinder concept, then more than ten years old.

Cheaper it may have been, but scarcely less powerful. The RGA's top speed, as measured at an official testing ground, was over 130mph. Large and heavy (at 538lb "dry"), the RGA, with new-style 120° crank, produced very considerable urge from as low as 2,000rpm, with a cruising speed of around 90mph equating to 5,000rpm. Low-speed running was unimpressive. The trouble apparently stemmed from the electronic ignition system which gave a leap in spark advance from 6° btdc at tickover to 34° btdc at 2,800rpm, the abrupt change resulting in a jerky power flow on the road.

Fuel consumption was heavy, averaging not more than about 35mpg and dropping into the 20s on hard-riding occasions.

Specification

RGA (1983) *Three-cylinder, ohc, four-stroke. 981cc (75 x 74mm). Five-speed gearbox. 4.4g fuel. Tyres, 100/90 x 18in (fr), 120/90 x 18in (r). 132mph.*

Formidable brakes of a 1983 triple.

Morini

Moto Morini was formed in 1937, a year after Alfonso Morini, the founder, began his commercial career in collaboration with Angelo Mattei, Mario Mazzetti and Giuseppi Massi. The original company was known as MM which, in view of the wealth of Ms available, ranks as self-denying discipline. MM stayed in business until 1964. Their golden years were pre-war when they won several Italian road-race titles and world records. (MM should not be confused with Moto Morini or with another Italian Morini company, once controlled by Alfonso's cousin, Franco, which produced small two-strokes.)

Alfonso broke with MM in 1937. In a new factory at Bologna he had his own foundry to produce cast-aluminium. Most of the plant was destroyed by bombing in the war, and it was late 1945 before he could offer a motor cycle for sale. It was a 125cc two-stroke single.

By 1949 Morini were turning out a 125 ohc four-stroke, giving 12bhp at 9,000rpm, that won the Italian 125 road-race title. But in the newly introduced world championships it was no match for the more developed Mondial. Morini's design had a single overhead camshaft controlled by a rightside chain, and hairpin springs for the valves. The crankcase was small, and a full-circle flywheel was mounted

In 1956 Morini's 175 Rebello was giving 22bhp at 9,000rpm.

externally. Having 52 x 58mm dimensions (as for the original two-stroke), the engine would rev prodigiously. Particular attention was paid to lubrication, the large oil tank being situated beneath the saddle, with a mechanical pump serving both delivery and scavenge; an oil-cooler was fitted to the rear of the tank. Initially the in-unit gearbox was fitted with three speeds, later increased to four. Front suspension was by a girder fork and there was a pivoted fork at the rear.

The lifetime of this useful engine extended to 1954, a change to dohc being introduced in 1952.

The compression ratio was raised from 9:1 to 10:1, and power output to 14bhp; top speed went up to 93mph. This was good enough to give the Morini a chance against the front runners in the 125cc class, Mondial and MV Agusta, but it was not until the end of 1952 that Morini began to make an impact on the international race scene, with a win in the final round of the world championship, in Spain. Victory gave the firm an inspiring send-off on the 1953 round of championship meetings, but MV and NSU (with their Rennfox) were too good for them; the best that Morini managed

was a second place in the Italian GP at Monza. By 1954 it was clear that the 125 was no longer competitive, so the factory changed its tactics and devoted more attention to the long-distance events, such as the Giro d'Italia and the Milano–Taranto.

Long defunct, these races generated a great deal of interest in the 1950s among Italian sports fans. Crowds packed the roadsides; victory paid big dividends in publicity for ordinary road machines. In fact roadsters were allowed to compete, but though Morini had a fine 175 in the Settebello, a new production racer was built specifically for the races. This was the Rebello. It had bore and stroke of 60 x 61mm, twin overhead camshafts, and was fitted at a slight forward inclination. Top power was 22bhp at 9,000rpm, giving a top speed of 105mph. The Rebello won the Milano–Taranto in 1955 and the Giro in 1955 and '56. Renowned, then, as a marathon racer, the Rebello also turned out to be an effective short-circuit machine. Bored and stroked to 66 x 69mm, for 250cc, it went up a capacity class and was entered in a few grands prix. Power output was 29bhp, and the Rebello served as a reasonable stand-in for the

Later the Rebello was enlarged to 250cc (69 × 69mm).

The purpose-built 250 racer, with 72 × 61mm engine developing 35bhp.

purpose-built 250 racer that was promised for 1958.

After a promising début, at the GP delle Nazioni, when Morini's Mendogni and Zubani proved too much for the MV-mounted duo of Ubbiali and Provini, the new 250 was relegated to underdog position in facing an improved MV and the new challenge of Honda. The choice was stark: Alfonso could indulge in more cylinders, more expense ... or go along the Carcano–Guzzi path of refining and lightening, in search of optimum performance. Given the state of Morini finances, there was little surprise when Morini undertook a programme of weight-cutting. Tarquinio Provini was prevailed on to sign for the firm for 1960 events. Alfonso set about tailoring the 250 to suit the new man. He went so far as to beat a recess in the tank top, to allow Provini to settle his chin in it while lying prone. The frame was completely redesigned. Straight tubes replaced the original, twin-loop structure; wheel size came down to 18in; the fuel tank was narrowed and lowered. An extremely efficient fairing was installed.

Power production was not, of course, ignored. Desmodromic valve operation was tried, and a four-valve head, and a special accelerator pump for fuel supply; all were abandoned as being too complex, or showing too marginal an improvement, to be worth while. Thus the engine remained basically as it had been designed: a 72 x 61mm 250 single with dohc operated by a gear train on the right, with twin-spark ignition and dry-sump lubrication. Power was inched up to 35bhp at 10,400rpm for a top speed of 137mph. In 1963 an extra 2bhp brought a further 5mph. Weight in the first two years of the machine's life was lowered from 251lb to 238lb, which allowed the brakes to be reduced by an

inch or so, to 8in at the front and 7in at the rear. There was talk at one stage of fitting disc brakes, as designed by Alfa Romeo, but nothing came of the idea.

This was the machine that came within a whisker of snatching the 1963 world championship title from mighty Honda, represented at the time by 60bhp fours and the riding talents of, in particular, Jim Redman of Rhodesia. Disappointed, and realising that the 1963 season had been the only chance of taking the crown, for Honda and the other Japanese firms were in process, almost weekly, it seemed, of increasing the power output of their costly engines, Morini confined factory competition to a programme of national meetings in which the 250 remained almost unbeatable until 1969, when Alfonso Morini died and racing was allowed to lapse.

On her father's death Gabrielle Morini took control of the small factory in Bologna. Her purpose, with the assistance of Gianni Marchetti and Franco Lambertini, was to revitalise the firm by introducing a range of up-to-date roadsters. The outcome of their efforts were the Morini vee-twins of today. Lambertini showed great ingenuity in basing all the engines of the new range –

The 250 dohc single in 1961.

125, 250, 350 and 500 – on much the same crankcase. Thus several models could be built at lowest tooling costs.

Simplicity was the main consideration. The Heron type of combustion chamber was chosen because it allowed the valves to be installed vertically, with a change in combustion shape, and volume, available at no greater expense than a switch in piston profile.

Making use of these engineering techniques, Morini have remained independent, and successful, through years which have seen other Italian manufacturers go to the wall, become nationalised, or be taken over by the controversial industrialist, de Tomaso.

Morini 250

Apparently termed the "Vice-less Vee" (in English?) by an Italian journalist, the 250 Morini was first imported into the UK in June 1980. It was, basically, like all the other Morinis, but writ rather small.

It had the usual 72° vee-twin engine with Heron combustion chambers; bore and stroke were 59 x 43.8mm, giving 239.5cc. Compression ratio was 11.7:1, there were twin Dellorto 22mm carburettors and electronic ignition, and the claimed power output was 26.8bhp (SAE) at 6,950rpm – enough, suggested the manufacturers and the English importers, for a top speed of 90mph. In the event, few testers managed more than 80 or thereabouts. Where the 250 scored, and fulfilled expectations, was in its frugal fuel-thirst, with 70–75mpg being available in quite brisk (60-ish) motoring.

Lighting, on a six-volt supply, was disappointing. Comfort, with hard suspension and over-thin seating, was minimal. Appearance, with gold-finished cast-alloy wheels, black engine and red paintwork for frame, mudguards, tank and panelling, was outstanding.

The retail price, as with the other Morinis, was high enough to make this 280lb 250 attractive only to the committed Morini follower who might, for reasons too obscure to go into here, be persuaded to step down in the modular range from 500 or 350.

Specification

250 2C (1980)   *Twin-cylinder, ohv, four-stroke. 239.5cc (59 x 43.8mm). Six-speed gearbox. 2.9g fuel. Tyres, 2.75 x 18in (fr), 3.00 x 18in (r). 80mph.*

Smallest of the roadster vee-twin Morinis is the six-speed 250.

Morini 3½

The "3½" title has always caused hesitation on the part of strangers to the model having some knowledge of the old system of RAC hp rating for motor cycles. In early days 3½ (hp) equated to 500cc, or thereabouts. So far as the Morini is concerned, the figures relate strictly to the model's 350cc.

Morini use the products of the best-known sections of the Italian ancillaries industry. Thus a 1980 3½ was equipped with Grimeca cast-alloy wheels and brakes, Ducati electrics, Dellorto carburettors, Marzocchi front forks and rear suspension, and Pirelli tyres.

No racer, the 3½ relies on individuality for appeal. Americans, particularly, can rate its speed capability in dismissive terms, as here ... "On a noon hour run to the hamburger stand the Morini rider would find himself revving and riding hard to keep pace with a variety of other,

Early 3½ with wire-spoke wheels and drum brakes.

The 3½ in 1979 with chrome-plated mudguards and exhaust system.

casually ridden machines." (In Europe, of course, with a paucity of hamburger stands, the Morini's noon-hour shortcomings are mercifully obscured.)

The 3½ has 62mm bore, 57mm stroke. The cylinders are set at 72° to each other and are slightly staggered, the front cylinder being to the right of the rear, to permit use of a common crankpin.

Four pushrods are operated from a belt-driven camshaft between the vee, with a rotor on the left side of the shaft. There is one coil per cylinder. All this is reasonably conventional. Where Morini design departs from the orthodox is in using Heron-style cylinder heads in which the compression ratio is mainly determined by the volume of piston-top depression. Cheap to produce, and with honoured precedents in the automotive world in Jaguar and Rover, the Heron layout has failed to find favour among motor cycle manufacturers other than Morini.

Another unusual feature is the rightside run for the final-drive chain, taken from a sprocket powered via helical-gear primary transmission.

Though Americans may not be enamoured of the 3½'s low-down power, some aspects of its specification have proved deeply fascinating to enthusiasts across the Atlantic. This is what *Cycle World* had to say about the starter layout: "By far the most elaborate piece of Rube Goldberg design in the entire unorthodox motor may be just inside the rightside alternator cover. For it is here that the electric starter assembly is lodged. The 12v starter motor is bolted longitudinally into the rear of the cover, its shaft at a right angle to the centre line of the crankshaft. The starter shaft drives a worm gear, where the power takes a 90 degree turn into a small sprocket which drives a chain to a larger sprocket on the starter clutch. The starter clutch is a centrifugal friction unit whose arms are thrown outward against the inside of a drum mounted on the alternator, when the starter is operated."

Got all that?

The point is that the starter works, at least when the bike is newish, and albeit with something of a *clang* as the button is pressed. However, Italians, both makers and consumers, being as pessimistic as Japanese manufacturers are confident, the Morini is equipped with a backup kickstarter. Instruments are by Veglia. The speedometer and rev-counter dials are large, easily read and, in the case of the former, rather "optimistic". The fuel tap has an electronic linkage, with a solenoid operating to permit fuel flow as the ignition is switched on.

The 3½ has considerable charm. It has endeared itself to many who have either long professed an aversion to what they see as the blandness of the modern Japanese motor cycle or have come round to this view on purchase, and experience, of one of these quirky 350s.

Specification

3½ (1980) *Vee-twin cylinder, ohv, four-stroke. 344cc (62 x 57mm). Six-speed gearbox. 3g fuel. Tyres, 100/90 x 19in (fr), 3.50 x 18in (r). 100mph.*

Morini Sahara

Previously "Camel"; for that was the first name bestowed on this trail version of the Morini 500. It was changed to Sahara when the looser connotations of the title, in a motor cycling sense especially, were made clear. The factory was disappointed, for Camel had seemed to convey precisely what the bike is good at: desert riding, at minimum running (consumption) cost.

The Sahara is long and tall, like the pure roadster 500, and the engines in both are practically identical. A one-piece forged crank runs on ball-bearing mains. The connecting rods have plain big-ends. Heron-design combustion chambers give a 11.2:1 compression ratio, and power output is quoted as 42bhp at 7,400rpm. The Maestro's electric starter is dispensed with; the kickstarter is on the left side and works through the layshaft, and thus neutral has to be engaged in starting.

Suspension is by Marzocchi. At the front, telescopic forks with 38mm stanchions give about 8in travel. At the

Basis for the Sahara was the roadster 500.

Many changes from the 500 were apparent in the Sahara, notably a reversion to small-diameter drum brakes.

rear, the unit has remote reservoirs for gas/oil damping and total movement is 6½-7in.

With competition in mind, even of a mild sort ... it should be made clear that the Sahara is not fitted for serious disputation with the current crop of purpose-built two-strokes ... the makers have arranged for easy removal of side panels, seat and fuel tank (the last on release of a single rubber loop).

Sitting high in the twin-loop frame, the engine is not equipped with sump protection, but as ground clearance is around 11in, none appears to be required. The lengthy wheelbase of 58in reflects the Sahara's road-bike roots and is a drawback when quick changes of direction are required.

Specification

Sahara (1982) *Twin-cylinder, ohv, four-stroke. 479cc (69 x 64mm). Six-speed gearbox. 3g fuel. Tyres, 3.00 x 21in (fr), 4.00 x 18in (r). 85–90mph.*

Moto Guzzi

Moto Guzzi were born during wartime conversations among World War I pilots Giorgio Parodi and Giovanni Ravelli and one of their mechanics, Carlo Guzzi. It was the last named, apparently, who directed talk away from whatever such Italian fighter aces usually discussed in off-duty moments to the subject of motor cycles. Guzzi planned to make motor cycles when the war was over; Ravelli, an ex-motor cycle racer, was interested; Parodi, apparently, couldn't think of anywhere else to go and usually ordered the drinks.

Ravelli was killed before the Armistice. Parodi and Guzzi teamed up, borrowed money from Giorgio's wealthy father, and set up their tiny factory at Mandello del Lario, on the shore of Lake Como. Parodi senior was made head of the company, and was assisted by his son; Carlo got down to designing motor cycles.

The prototype Guzzi – first known as the GP (Guzzi Parodi) – was built in 1919, though production did not begin until 1921 when a workforce of ten turned out a total of 17 motor cycles. The design was unconventional. The engine was a single-cylinder 500 laid flat and in unit with a three-speed gearbox. It and the rest of the motor cycle are described in some detail in the first entry in this section.

In 1924 the 500 won the European championship at Monza and in 1926 was joined by a 250cc version having a bore and stroke of 68 x 68mm. Although both machines were taken to the Isle of Man that year as part (with Bianchi and Garelli) of the Italian invasion of that English bastion of road-racing, it was the 250 that attracted the greater attention, through an episode that demonstrated some striking aspects of the Italian character. Pietro Gherzi was to ride both Senior and Junior Guzzis and arrived in Manxland a couple of weeks ahead of official practice. Every day he set out to learn the circuit. Sometimes he covered as many as five laps, retaking difficult corners time after time, before retiring,

exhausted, to his bed. The result of this dedication was second place in the Junior – followed almost immediately by disqualification when it was discovered that the spark plug he had used in the race was of a different make from that fitted at the weigh-in. He had, it appeared, been warned about this breach of regulations; his ingenious ... some said ingenuous ... excuse was that, as a visitor, he expected special consideration. This explanation did not endear him to officialdom but nothing could detract from his popularity with spectators, who showed their feelings by booing the stewards and carrying the emotional racer shoulder high to the rostrum.

His reputation was made for posterity at the end of the week when he took the 500 through the opening lap of the Senior at 68mph; crashed, and carried on, in worsening pain, to his eventual, reluctant, retirement.

There were, therefore, no TT victories for Guzzis in this first visit to the Isle of Man.

In 1928 the touring models were given a refinement that the racers did not possess: a spring frame. Triangulated chain stays were pivoted immediately to the rear of the seat tube, the lower set being attached to two long rods terminating in a spring box beneath the engine. The springs were totally enclosed, and immersed in oil. External friction dampers were interposed between the rear of the pivoted fork and the seat sub-frame.

Guzzi conducted their development programme at a frantic pace. For example: following the Model 14, they built and raced an across-the-frame supercharged horizontal four (in 1931), then developed two new roadsters for 1932, one a 174cc single, the other a 500cc horizontal transverse three...and still found time to construct a classic racer, the 120° vee-twin, which was released in 1933.

Compared with the later success of the vee-twin, the blown four rates as a failure. (On its first outing, at Monza, tar was sucked into the intake and clogged the supercharger.) In company with the singles, the four's engine drove through

This 1929 racing 500 (88 × 83mm) Guzzi has a bronze cylinder head with four valves and a long induction pipe curved through almost 90°. Camshaft drive is by Guzzi's customary shaft and bevels. The oil container on top of the fuel tank holds 10 pints. Foot-change mechanism is a later addition.

Close-up of the 1929 500. Frame is extremely robust but heavy.

Another (two-valve) 500, from the 30s, this one rear-sprung and equipped with factory-contrived foot-change control.

Two-valve 250 with race-style oil tank.

In 1939 the 68 × 68mm 250 was supercharged, with the blower mounted above the gearbox and linked to a large balance chamber over the cylinder. Fast but not entirely reliable, it was unable to match the phenomenal (albeit normally aspirated) Benelli ridden by Ted Mellors.

an in-unit gearbox: but unlike the earlier machines, the cylinders were tilted, for cooler running of the exhaust valves. Bore and stroke were 56 x 50mm. The crankshaft ran on three roller bearings, with ducts in the shaft for pressure lubrication. Short pushrods actuated two valves per head, with hairpin springs for closure. An unusual oil-cooling radiator was positioned just beneath the steering head, with lubricant stored in a separate container. The intake system was labyrinthine, the carburettor being well back from the engine, in the region of the rear mudguard, and supplying mixture through a Cozette supercharger (with individual lubrication) and plenum chamber. The result was an under-tank area apparently filled to capacity with cylinders, pipes and cables, in a manner foretelling the layout of the even more complicated multis of the postwar era.

Much simpler, cleaner in line – and far more race-worthy – was the 500cc vee-twin which, complete with spring frame, aroused much speculation, but little concern, among TT rivals when it first appeared, as Stanley Woods' mount, in the Isle of Man in 1935. Woods won the Senior race on the twin after achieving a resounding victory, on a Guzzi single, in the 250cc Lightweight race, when he humiliated the Rudges

that had dominated the previous year's event.

The vee-twin was a tribute to Carlo Guzzi's return to a more reasonable state of mind, following the heady excesses of the supercharged multi. He realised early that the 250 single, with outside flywheel and compact crank-case, lent itself to doubling up: a further cylinder could be tacked on, with minimum complication, to the rear, pointing up to the saddle. As constructed, the second cylinder, being indeed a straightforward duplicate of the original, had its exhaust at the front, and carburettor to the rear. The engine was in unit with a four-speed gearbox, and many of the detail features, such as use of bevel drive for the oh camshafts, and hairpin valve springs, followed the pattern laid down for the single.

By 1937 Guzzi had increased their roadster showing to include a 250 horizontal single, the Ardetta, with pressed-steel frame and coil ignition; a sports version, named the Egretta and claimed to be good for 100mph; and a production-racer version of the 500 single, known as the Condor.

In immediate pre-war years Guzzi ingenuity was manifested in a supercharged three-cylinder 500 racer that was intended to give the firm a

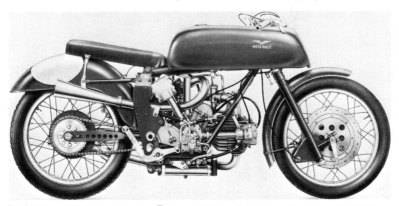

This 1949 vee-twin was developed from a 1933 design that went on to win the 1935 IoM Senior TT. Essentially two 250 engines, with individual crankpins phased at 120°, it started life producing 44bhp at 7,000rpm. With further modifications to frame and brakes, but very little change to the engine, it remained a formidable competitor into the 1950s.

better chance in tussles with the blown BMWs and Gileras that were beginning to trounce the vee-twin with disheartening regularity. Questioned as to why he had not persevered with a four-cylinder design, Carlo Guzzi said that, though mindful of the four's advantages in torque and balance, he was won over to the three by the opportunity it presented of keeping weight and bulk within more reasonable limits. There was not much frame, in the accepted sense, but what there was of it was fabricated mainly in aluminium. Light-alloy was used for cylinders, heads, brake drums and wheel rims.

Bore and stroke were 59 x 60mm. The cranks were at 120°, while the cylinders inclined at 45°. Twin ohc and central spark plugs were other familiar Guzzi features of an engine said to produce 70–80bhp. The outbreak of World War II prevented final development.

In 1946 Moto Guzzi · returned to "civilian" motor cycling though not, for the time being, to racing. After a brief flirtation with cyclemotors, the factory wheeled out four roadgoing models: a 65cc single-cylinder two-stroke, a three-wheeler, and two horizontal-engine singles similar to the pre-war machines. The smaller of these, the 250 Airone, formed the basis of the Albatross racer, and the 500 GTS had a racing counterpart also, designed for use in Italian formula events in which a weight limit of 275lb had been set for 500cc machines. This was to become the renowned Gambalunga (long legs) – a reference to its stroke measurement which, at 90mm, though modest in comparison with, say, a Norton's 100mm, impressed Italian race fans as being, somehow, exceptional. Whether the bike deserved its initial fame may be debatable; what is beyond dispute is that the Gambalunga's reputation became secure through an outstanding record of race successes over the years. Light, reliable, and surprisingly fast, despite the engine's modest power, the Gambalunga was a favourite among

The 1949 500 Gambalunga single, which produced 35bhp at little more than 5,000rpm.

The 250 Gambalunghino of the same year.

Italian racing men. When the 250 was improved, with a 500-style frame, the Albatross title was dropped in favour of (of course) Gambalunghino.

As Guzzi racers progressed through a series of victories on the track in the late 40s, detractors – mainly British – began to hint at vaguely sinister reasons behind their success. At first it was said that Guzzi had developed the racers during the war. Then, as this was disproved, the critics declared there must be government backing for the firm. This, too, was untrue. What the Guzzi race department had was an extremely talented director in Giulio Carcano. More than talented, as will be made clear.

Moto Guzzi celebrated their venture into international racing in 1947 with a one-two victory in the IoM Lightweight TT. Controversial though it was, with victory in dispute at the time and for long after between Maurice Cann and Manliff Barrington (the latter being credited as winner), this event sparked off a series of five class wins for Guzzi during the next six years in the Isle of Man, with world championship titles in 1949, '51 and '52. All were achieved with the single-cylinder 250, as continually improved by Carcano, and finally enlarged, at equipe leader Fergus Anderson's suggestion, to more than 300cc, to enable it to compete in 350cc-class racing. It began in early 1953 as a 320 (the 250's bore and stroke being increased to 72 x 80mm) and before mid-season had grown, with 75 x 79mm measurements, to full 350cc size, in which form it went on to win that year's class championship, and bring to an end a six-year domination by the two major British factories.

A 1952-type Gambalunghino with four-gallon tank extending beyond the steering head. Power of this 260lb racer was 25bhp. Rear suspension control had been changed to vertical struts.

Fergus Anderson racing a Gambalunghino at Ferrara in 1949. Contemporary talk of eyebrow-raising speeds for the 250 Guzzis was contradicted by Anderson, who was able to quote timed autostrada tests carried out by Dr Giorgio Parodi which revealed a two-way average of just over 100mph.

In 1953 the 250 was stretched first to 320cc and then to a full-size 350, in which form (Anderson up) it won the world championship that year.

Fergus Anderson on the 350 single in 1954; the early proboscis streamlining had been replaced by a speed-boosting "dustbin".

A revised frame was a feature of the 1956 350 that achieved yet another world championship, in the hands of Bill Lomas.

It took 350cc titles every year up to 1957, often giving away 10-20 per cent in power to its rivals, but invariably scoring through reliability, light weight and extreme handleability. Carcano's crusade to shed excess poundage became legendary. He replaced the iron cylinder liner with a hard-chrome coating, double valve springs with single coils, the 14mm spark plug with a 10mm; even (though this may be apocryphal) left the fairing unpainted! The wind-tunnel-developed fairing was bolted direct to the frame, saving the weight of support struts. By 1957 the 350 had undergone a change of bore and stroke, for a radically oversquare ratio (before reverting to "long-stroke" 75 x 79mm figures); in that year it was producing 38bhp at 8,000rpm and top speed was given as more than 140mph.

In the 500cc class Carcano had not been so successful. The vee-twin, successor to the single, was unreliable. Carcano's would-be replacement, a longitudinal four, with shaft final drive, was not fast enough. The stage was set for the V8 as described later in this

Prototype of the 1955 350 (75 × 79mm) single had the 35bhp engine carried in a new multi-tube frame and enveloped by a dustbin fairing. Later versions were equipped with a low, transverse fuel container, a dummy tank being retained in the usual position to support the rider.

The 1954 longitudinal 500 four with rear shaft drive that proved a disappointment.

section. When it, and racing, were abandoned in 1957 Moto Guzzi had won more than 3,300 international races, 11 IoM TTs and 14 world championships, and had taken 134 world speed records.

In the roadster field Moto Guzzi were unable to come up with successes to rival their race machines. The best they managed was the 500cc Falcone (1950–67) which, with outside-flywheel, horizontal engine, produced plenty of easy,

undemanding power. There were, of course, other models of some merit which made a less than outstanding impact; the Galletto scooter, for one, which had the misfortune, with its ungainly appearance, to be measured against the aesthetically superior Vespa and Lambretta. No matter that the Galletto was better made, and a better all-round road machine; a scooter fashion of bulbous bodywork and

The 150cc ohv single, with outside flywheel, powering the excellent Galletto scooter.

The 500 Falcone single, manufactured in quantity from 1950 to 1967.

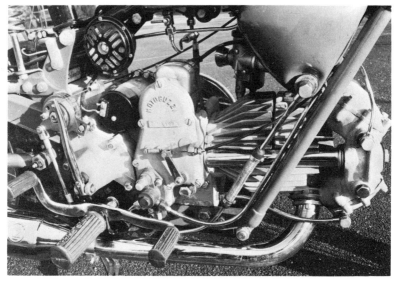

Engine of the Falcone was mainly unchanged throughout the model's life.

The reborn Falcone of 1970, few examples of which escaped from Italy, had innovations such as electric starting, internal flywheel, twin silencers and twin-leading-shoe front brake.

miniature wheels had been set by the Big Two, and any two-wheeler in the same market, and out for big sales, had to conform. The Galletto failed on several counts, having 17in wheels, motor cycle-style suspension and angular bodywork; and not forgetting its mechanically noisy but decidedly efficient four-stroke engine.

During its lifetime the Falcone spawned a model for police and military use known as the Alce. When this machine, with its outside-flywheel ... "bacon-slicer" ... engine, finally proved unable to meet government requirements, Guzzi had no alternative but to lay down a new design. Or modify an existing one. The latter course offering a quicker, cheaper solution, there was little surprise in Guzzi's ingenious adaptation of a vee-twin engine developed a decade earlier for use in a light, four-wheeled vehicle employed in forestry work. Drawing on lessons gained from experiments with an all-indirect gearbox and shaft final drive, as featured in the racing four, Guzzi evolved the now-familiar transverse layout. Arranged in this fashion, and maintaining a 90° angle between the cylinders, the vee-twin displayed advantages in balance, cooling and ground clearance. A glance at the original V7, with its bulky dynamo, car-type starter and distributor, and generally unlovely looks, underlines the development which within a few years produced the rakish Le Mans. Carcano

played a part in keeping the V7's weight down, by specifying light-alloy cylinders with chrome-plated bores, but most credit for later improvements belongs to consultant Lino Tonti, who eventually settled at Mandello when Carcano retired.

Developed through 757, 844 and 949cc, and then the other way, down through 498 to 349cc, the one-time V7 layout has, in the 1980s, a near-40 year pedigree. Following the takeover by Alessandro de Tomaso, in 1953, Moto Guzzi extended their range to include two-strokes and ohc multis matching parallel machines produced in the Benelli sector of de Tomaso's empire.

Moto Guzzi Sport 14

There is little about pre-World War II Italian motor cycles in this book. Perhaps the Sport 14 may stand as a not untypical example of the big, sporting single that pleased the heart of the Italian enthusiast of the 20s and 30s, in much the way that an ohc Norton was treasured by his English contemporary.

It was built from 1922 to 1930, with few major changes in a run of 11,000 machines. It made history because of its unorthodox yet functional lines. It was conceived during World War I by Carlo Guzzi and a prototype was built in 1919. Having advanced "oversquare" dimensions, the engine was laid flat in the frame, with the crankcase covers

Early V7 Guzzi with 700cc, 50bhp engine.

extended to conceal the primary drive, clutch, gearbox and magneto drive. It had fully automatic lubrication, with external feed and scavenge pipes, a single overhead camshaft driven by shaft and bevels, four valves and twin-plug ignition. The external flywheel became a Guzzi hallmark. The frame was in the form of a full cradle, with double down tubes. Power was around 17bhp and top speed 80mph.

However, the specification was too complicated to permit of a reasonable selling price. When the production version appeared in 1921, under the name of 500 Normale, several changes were evident. A two-valve head had been installed, the inlet being at the side and the overhead exhaust pushrod-operated. With single ignition and general detuning, the engine gave 12bhp at around 3,500rpm and top speed dropped to 55mph. But it had virtues unknown to the complex original. Reliability had been improved and there were fewer servicing requirements. The tubular frame was simplified – and cheapened – by introduction of pressed-steel sections at the rear; this was a temporary measure, however, for within a year the management had repented and reinstated the more expensive tubular layout.

Carlo Perelli, a commentator on Italian motor cycling of long standing, details the outstanding features of the Sport 14.

Among the surprising aspects were the 88 x 82mm bore and stroke, for lower piston speed and better breathing, the horizontal cylinder, for better cooling, the backward-running engine, eliminating not only an intermediate gear between the crankshaft and the clutch drum, to get the rotation "right" again, but also contributing to a natural oil throw in the direction of the upper cylinder bore.

The side/overhead valve layout was a compromise, for it was clear that all-ohv would be superior. In those days, however, valves were prone to breakage. If they were in the head, when they broke they would fall into the bore. Carlo Guzzi put the exhaust valve, in need of more cooling, in the head; and in order to have, as he believed, a more rational combustion-chamber shape. (The idea of a variation in valve position was not new, of course, but usually it was the inlet that was installed in the head.)

The oil tank, under the steering head, was well cooled, with a double pump – a rarity in its day – giving efficient circulation.

Weight was low, at 240lb, as was the centre of gravity, which made the Sport 14 a good handler. It had vast pulling power, extraordinary docility (not surprising, with a 4:1 compression ratio) and, because of the damping effect of the large flywheel, practically no vibration.

The Sport 14, a pleasing big single.

Specification

Sport 14 (1928) *Single-cylinder, oh/sv, four-stroke. 492cc (88 x 82mm). Three-speed gearbox. 2.5g fuel. Tyres, 4.00 x 19in. 55–60mph.*

Moto Guzzi Zigolo

The Zigolo began life with a 98cc engine when Moto Guzzi, at the time the biggest of the Italian makers, were closely identified with a horizontal engine layout. The Zigolo, therefore, had its two-stroke engine, with suitably horizontal finning, projecting forward in the manner of one of the company's racers. No other racing connection was apparent – with the possible exception of the rear springing, with large, hand-controlled friction dampers. The use of pressed-steel panelling, suggesting a monocoque construction, was distinctly ahead of the times; in fact, the panelling was almost precisely *that*, having no role as a load-bearer, for underneath was a large-diameter spine frame. The rear pivoted fork was constructed in oval tubing, with shock and rebound springing controlled by centrally mounted rubber units. At the front, the telescopic fork was of conventional design, though incorporating a rather unusual method of quick release for the wheel spindle. The engine had 50 x 50mm bore and stroke, ran on a 6:1 compression ratio and inhaled from a Dellorto carburettor via a rotary valve on the right side of the engine shaft. That the system was effective is shown in published performance figures for the Zigolo which give top speed as 45mph. Not a dazzling speed, admittedly, but well up to two-stroke class standards for the capacity.

The Zigolo was popular in Italy but was no competition for Vespa-style runabouts abroad.

Ignition and lighting current came from a Marelli flywheel magneto-generator on the crankshaft; access to the coil – and the carburettor – was provided by a detachable panel in the left side of the bodywork.

The three-speed gearbox, mounted in unit with the engine, and with a multi-plate "wet" clutch driven by helical gears, was controlled by foot.

This early Zigolo, popular in Italy, was a disappointing seller in the UK; as, indeed, were later variants with larger engines. It was born at a time when powered two-wheelers had to be either conventional motor cycles or the newly-popular scooter. The Zigolo attempted a bridge between the two. Conservative-minded Britons, still befuddled by scooter excesses, were not impressed.

Specification

Zigolo (1953) *Single-cylinder, two-stroke. 98cc (50 x 50mm). Three-speed gearbox. 3g fuel. Tyres, 2.50 x 19in. 45mph.*

Moto Guzzi Lodola 175

The smallest, and earliest, Lodola imported into the UK was of 175cc. Later versions were stretched to 235cc. Its appearance, judging by British standards of the late 1950s, suggested a swept volume nearer 350cc, for finning on both cylinder and head of the engine, forwardly inclined at 45°, was massive. Examination of the Lodola by anybody unversed in Guzzi lore would have given no indication of the method of valve operation. There were no signs of pushrod tunnels, or camshaft-drive enclosure, in the facade of close-pitch finning. In fact, it was an ohc layout, with drive to the camshaft by chain.

A duplex cradle frame with wide-spaced front tubes carried pivoted-fork rear springing and a vestige of enclosure, by sheet-steel panelling, in the under-dualseat area. The front fork was telescopic, with hydraulic damping, and the valanced mudguard was clamped to the sprung section of the fork, presenting a very neat appearance; except, that is, on those occasions when the fork was extended, resulting in an unsightly gap between tyre and guard.

The gearbox had four speeds and was mounted in unit with the engine; gear selection was by the favoured continental method of a rocking pedal on the right side. Ratios had not been doctored to suit UK conditions ... understandably, for exports formed at the time a negligible part of Moto Guzzi's business ... and, consequently, tended to leave the Lodola rider, in pre-M1 days, longing for a lower-ratio top gear. Third gear,

Fairing off, the V8 reveals the formidable complexity of its power plant, tight-packed into a fairly conventional frame incorporating an oil-carrying spine. With gear primary drive, the engine runs backwards, the gearbox having a crossover drive from near- to off-side.

however, was good for nearly 55mph and was much used on undulating secondary roads.

The rocking pedal gear-change was a "racing" affectation. British motor cycles of the 1930s had been on occasion thus equipped, to give a "TT" look. The compiler – and, probably, most other English riders – raised on the conventional layout, never took to the idea. A proper racing crouch might have made all the difference. When one rode in the usual upright way the right foot seemed to lack the necessary flexibility. It was easier to ignore the rear part of the pedal. The only loss was any hope of a Kiwi glitter.

Specification

Lodola (1958) *Single-cylinder, ohc, four-stroke. 175cc (62 x 57.8mm). Four-speed gearbox. 2.5g fuel. Tyres, 2.50 x 18in (fr), 3.00 x 17in. 61mph.*

Moto Guzzi V8

The outstanding figure among the motor cycle engineers of the postwar era, in the view of race commentator V.H. Willoughby, who had an acquaintance with most of them, was Giulio Carcano of Moto Guzzi. He was, said Willoughby, a genius. He it was who designed the watercooled 500 V8 following a halcyon period for Guzzi during which he shepherded a number of old-fashioned singles to a half-dozen world championships.

Many years before the V8 saw light of day a British vee-twin, the Brough Superior, with 8.75 JAP, had been reckoned as having two of everything. It had two carburettors, two magnetos and two exhausts. The numbers game moved into a fresh dimension when the V8 came along. There were eight carburettors, eight ignition coils, eight exhaust pipes; a multitude of oil lines and water pipes; a tacho reading to 12,000 rpm. It could reach speeds nearer 180 than 170mph.

The V8's design was laid down in 1954. Carcano had seen a widespread improvement in handling and pene-tration among the race machines fielded by rival manufacturers. These were the very advantages that he had laboured to exploit – successfully – on behalf of Guzzi's relatively low-powered racers. And it was obvious that these advantages were being eroded. The future, he reasoned, lay with *power*. Hence the V8.

Ready to race in 1955–56, it proved a match for Gilera's championship-winning four. But when Moto Guzzi (with Gilera) withdrew from international racing, it was retired, along with all the Guzzi singles.

In authentic story-book style, Carcano is reputed to have sketched a layout for the V8 over the remains of a meal that took place during the 1954 Spanish GP. Carcano, already a veteran of multi-cylinder design, with a 500 in-line four that had proved only moderately successful, could see only one way to beat the all-conquering Gilera and its upstart rival, the MV Agusta. More cylinders, leading to increased rpm, would do the trick, he reasoned; and a V8 could be, additionally, both slimmer and lower than the transverse fours.

Paul Schilling, the American writer, has written an account of the birth and brief life of the V8. He was assisted by Bill Lomas, twice a world champion on 350 Guzzi singles, who rode the V8 on several occasions.

Carcano had no army of technicians, teams of specialists, or computers. He had his experience, and the help of 11 people in the racing department. The factory sanctioned the design in September 1954; by Christmas the castings were being machined; in February 1955 the V8 ran for the first time. In April it was tested at Monza.

Dimensions were 44 x 41mm for each 62cc cylinder. Each bank of cylinders had dohc. Six spur gears, in a case on the right side, actuated the camshafts, which connected with the valves via bucket tappets. Heads and block were in light-alloy, and watercooled, the heads by means of cast-in water jackets. The drive for the water pump came off the camshaft gear train. The radiator was mounted low, forward of the front down tubes. The oil pump was triggered by the camshaft drive train, and the single top tube of the frame doubled as an oil

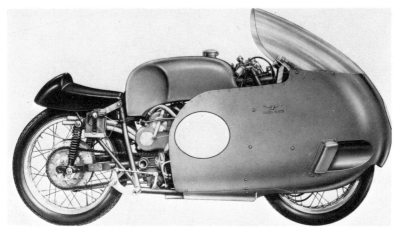

With fairing fitted the 70-80bhp V8 weighed 320lb, "dry". Slots in the nose duct air to the front brake and the radiator.

Wind-tunnel-tested, the V8's enclosure presents a frontal aspect decidedly slimmer than that of the transverse fours fielded by Gilera and MV Agusta.

reservoir for the dry-sump engine. The crankshaft was supported in five roller bearings, the crank throws at 180° with, on each throw, two connecting rods running side by side. After initial tests, the lower end was modified in various ways in search of greater reliability.

Two large housings, each containing a set of four points, were positioned on the left side of the two inlet camshafts. Flanking the radiator, and specially protected, were eight ignition coils, four per side, to fire 10mm spark plugs. Two six-volt batteries provided power for ignition; there was no generator. Eight 20mm Dellorto carburettors, with long intake trumpets, were crowded between the cylinder banks like – as Schilling memorably puts it – fingers in a pair of tightly folded hands. Between the contact-breaker housings were two float chambers, one for each quartet of carburettors. Four small exhausts for the front bank of cylinders were trailed under the engine; those for the rear cylinders were taken rearward between the frame tubes and the rear tyres. There were no megaphones. Primary drive was by gears in a cover on the left side to a dry clutch. Experiments with both six- and four-speed gearboxes were settled in favour of fewer gears, for the power band, stretching from 7,000 to 12,000rpm, rendered the six-speeder superfluous.

Lomas recalled for Schilling the first occasion when the engine was run on the dynamometer. The very first power reading was 62bhp at the rear wheel. One mechanic, Pommi, did all the V8 engine building. Carcano himself carried out, or supervised, the engine testing. Never was it necessary to scratch for more horsepower.

The engine was mounted in a relatively conventional duplex frame. Schilling describes it..."The pivot boss for the rear pivoted fork was part of the transmission casing; the engine/transmission package bolted into the twin-down tube frame, which cradled the engine. The enormous top tube ran back from the steering head over the engine; behind the engine the rear cradle tubes arose, turned 90 degrees in and joined up with the top member under the saddle."

Lomas felt that the handling problems arose because of the low weight of the racer, at 326lb, and because the carburation was a little hit or miss, caused by having the float chambers on the left side of the engine. As the machine was leaned into a corner, carburation would be either weak or rich, never consistent. The leading-link front suspension may have been unsuitable, in some respects; certainly, according to Lomas, the tyres of the day were at their limit in coping with the power.

By the end of 1955 the V8 was faster than the rival fours. An increase in carburettor and exhaust pipe size, and raising the compression ratio to over 10:1, contributed to a power increase to 72bhp at 12,000rpm.

Connecting-rod failures dogged the early outings of the V8. The original layout of a one-piece crankshaft with two-piece rods on crowded rollers collapsed, as did the first modification, which relied on split-cage rollers and plain bearings. Finally a solution was found in the use of a built-up crankshaft with Hirth-style couplings. This was complicated, and expensive, but it was then possible to employ one-piece rods on normal rollers.

In two grands prix during the early part of the 1956 season Lomas demonstrated that the V8 was comfortably faster than

Surtees' MV or Duke's Gilera. He did not win either race (retiring through different troubles) but the potential of the new racer was abundantly clear. However, its race record was to prove a disappointment, with only a couple of wins in Italy to show for the months of steady development that had culminated in rear-wheel power of 82bhp. A publicity stunt on a closed section of the Appian Way produced world records and a timed kilometre at 178mph. All the races it contested, jockeyed by a selection of riders deputising for an injured, sidelined, Lomas, turned out to be tantalising near-misses. Then, in October 1957, Moto Guzzi pulled out of racing. Lomas retired. The V8 was packed away, never to race again.

Specification

V8 (1954) *Eight-cylinder, dohc, four-stroke. 496cc (44 x 41mm). Four-speed gearbox. 7.5g fuel. Tyres, 3.00 x 2in (fr), 3.50 x 20in (r). 160–180mph.*

Moto Guzzi V1000

An inveterate, expert observer of the Italian motor cycle scene thought that the Moto Guzzi V1000 Hydro Convert, introduced in 1975, represented "perhaps the most significant step in motorcycle design to have seen the light of day since the adoption of the chain as a drive medium." The words are D.L. Minton's. No matter what others assumed about this third-generation Guzzi ... in the main, that it was an "automatic" ... Minton pinned it down as a *gearless* machine, having affinity with a DAF car or a Triumph Tina scooter, the major difference between these and the V1000 lying in the hydraulic drive system of the latter.

With this gearless transmission were partnered coupled brakes, a brilliant basic specification – and, in the usual Italian fashion, shamefully inadequate detail items.

Minton found that it was the sheer simplicity of riding that struck him most forcibly. "The relaxed mental and physical attitudes allowed by the woofling twin [he wrote] is probably a greater part of the title 'luxury tourer' than

Riding "like an over-indulged potentate" on a V1000.

the direct advantages of the mechanical sophistication of the machine. Mind you, there's nothing better than prodding a button early in the morning and, without a single further move, riding off by nominally easing back the twistgrip, then sitting like an overindulged potentate for the rest of the day while the world drifts past, without lifting a finger to help yourself!"

On a motorway, or any fast main road, riding this big Guzzi was little different from speeding on an ordinary motor cycle. It was in traffic conditions that the advantages of the transmission system came home. Owners were said to arrive at their journey's end in a better state of mind than traffic-threading had ever previously allowed. The experience was likened to riding, at one and the same time, a super-simple moped and a powerful motor cycle. The combination amounted to an unbeatable partnership. Never boring, surprisingly, but supremely restful. (Strange, then, that the Guzzi did not head a general move to automatics ... gearless machines.)

The secret was in what used loosely to be termed a fluid flywheel, as found in rather grand cars of a bygone day such

as Daimler and Armstrong Siddeley. In the case of the Guzzi, though, instead of locking-up solid at just over tickover speeds, the hydraulic system remained fluid throughout. Thanks to the characteristics displayed by all fluids under pressure, at low speeds the toleration of the transmission medium was high – consequently, power transfer was uniquely smooth. This meant that starting was progressive, far more so than with any manually controlled system: thus, it was next to impossible to break rear-wheel traction on a wet city street even under hard acceleration.

As engine speed went up so the hydraulic connection increasingly displayed the characteristics of a conventional machine, which meant that engine braking once more became useful, and twistgrip movement manifested itself more immediately at the rear wheel.

Acceleration was not fast; but because only a single action was required of the rider – at the throttle – it was a matter of acquiring very little experience before the advantages of the fluid flywheel could be very usefully exploited. Whacking open the throttle

The automatic Convert was introduced in 1975.

produced results quickly enough to satisfy all but the out-and-out sports buff, and because no pauses were called for during the otherwise inevitable lag on clutch operation and gear changing, what appeared initially to be a ponderous getaway was transformed very smartly into a sort of "elastic band" acceleration process, unbroken and relentless. The best results were produced by standing hard on the footbrake, winding open the throttle till the bike began shuddering in protest, feeling as if it were sweating torque at every joint, and then letting go. Then it *leapt!* But still with the same uncanny controllability. When the Guzzi was used in this manner, conventional machines found it no easy task to keep pace.

A lower gear ratio was available for semi-emergency use, such as traffic-jam crawling or off-road hill-climbing ... not that the lengthy 600lb bike invited much of the latter ... and it was very useful in retaining the higher engine speed "positive-drive" characteristics at low road speeds, when required; but in general that 20 per cent drop in ratio was seldom used. The factory claimed a top speed of 84mph, "low" gear engaged, and independent tests supported this; but 70mph was as high as most owners liked to go. Top speed in "high" was 110mph. A constant throttle opening appeared to give a pretty constant road

"Square-slide" Dellortos and knee-protectors.

speed, held, presumably, by the varying load applied to the hydraulic fluid, which governed engine speed, allowing it to increase on heavy loading and fall back under a light load, thanks to its inbuilt tolerance.

Minton, for one, was bowled over by the system ... mentally, that is, for as far as can be ascertained, he had no on-the-road scrapes during his thousand miles with a Convert. He thought, back in the mid-70s (erroneously, as it has turned out), that other manufacturers would be bound to follow suit with systems offering similar facilities, although he doubted that anybody would be able to match de Tomaso's layout, "no doubt patented up

buttons, switches, controls, rivets, nuts and bolts – and indeed all subsidiary parts – functioned perfectly, the equivalent items on the Guzzi were disappointing in their manufacturing and performance quality.

Old-style cars with fluid flywheels were fitted with safety devices to protect unwitting owners from racing off, in gear, at a press of the button. Something of the same sort had been devised for the V1000, where firing up on open throttles was potentially even more hazardous. Guzzi therefore wired two cutout

Another variation on the luxury theme – the California model with manual-control gearbox.

to its eyeballs by some of Italy's top legal brains".

The V1000's departure from standard practices did not end with the transmission system. It was awash with gimmicks. Individually, they were daunting, but their combined performance contributed powerfully towards a grand ride, free and uncluttered. But some detail points, as mentioned earlier, were unsatisfactory; and two were downright bad.

Where, say, a Honda Gold Wing's

switches into the circuit. One was mounted on the clutch cable, close to the clutch; unless the clutch lever on the handlebar was operated, disengaging the drive, and leaving the engine free to rev without transmitting power, the circuit was broken. This was the theory. But it was not supported by the ease with which dirt and water found their way past the skimpy plastic covering for the device, and promptly immobilised the machine. As there was no kickstarter, and as the transmission would not spin the engine during a run-and-dump attempt, life with the V1000 could be ... well, frustrating.

Then there was the prop stand. Unlike many, it was long, easily accessible to the rider while normally seated, and provided a secure support for the machine, not least because it incorporated a simple but ingenious ... the two are compatible, aren't they? ... lever activating a cable clamping the rear-brake pads on to the disc. There was a strong spring on hand, to snap it into place, both on and off. The stop pawl on the stand was short, and butted against a ⅛in steel pressing clinched by a rivet. The inertia built up by the weight on the stand along its considerable length, and the strength of the spring, was not small. Inevitably the rivet-head crimping would pull through, the stand would bend, the bike would topple over, and (usually) the stand switch would be broken....

In fairness, it must be said that others among the Guzzi's list of unconventional "twiddly bits" worked rather better. The electric fuel tap, energised by the ignition circuit – meaning that, effectively, there was no need for the rider to touch the tap – never gave trouble, and nor did the choke, which was of the sort that did not increase engine speed while enriching mixture.

Finally, there was the coupled braking system which, while not restricted to this particular model – it was, and is, a standard fitting on all Guzzis – was thrown into greater prominence by the transmission system of the V1000, with its inevitable lack of engine-braking effect.

It was introduced by Moto Guzzi with the aim of reducing the potential for rider error by just about eliminating unwanted, or unwarranted, wheel-locking. With this setup there was no need for fine co-ordination between power-on and front- and rear-brake application. On the V1000 the drive medium absorbed the effect of thoughtless, or hasty, throttle changes comfortably and the coupled brakes reacted more powerfully, though less fiercely, than conventional units. Deliberate provocation, by stamping on the pedal, say, was the only way to lock the rear wheel, and the front one never

locked. Depressing the right side foot pedal stimulated simultaneously a (claimed) 75/25 per cent hydraulic effort into the front left disc and matching rear brake. The front left disc could be applied alone, by use of the usual lever control on the handlebar. After an initial riding spell, most Guzzi owners found themselves ignoring this facility, and using the foot control exclusively.

Specification

V1000 (1975) *Twin-cylinder, ohv, four-stroke. 949cc (88 x 78mm). Two-speed gearbox; torque converter. 5.25g fuel. Tyres, 4.10 x 18in. 110mph.*

Moto Guzzi 250TS

By the time the TS came along, in the 70s, the Japanese had creamed off the lucrative 250cc sector of the UK market. Honda had their best-selling four-stroke; other members of the Big Four trailed – but not very far behind – with speedy, reliable two-strokes. That the TS was a two-stroke was somewhat surprising, for Moto Guzzi's reputation rested very firmly on the big vee-twins with which they had regained prominence in the motor cycle world.

The Gilera Arcore (described elsewhere in these pages) was almost overengineered in comparison with competitors among the Japanese, resulting in telling handicaps of inferior speed and an inflated selling price. Guzzi's 250, however, alongside Honda, Suzuki and Kawasaki equivalents (if not Yamaha's speedy RD), was of spartan build and had a sparkling performance. It could not, unfortunately, deliver the second, seemingly more important, part of the equation that had enabled the Japanese to crush the likes of the Arcore. Despite its simple specification, it was not cheap.

Where the Japanese 250s weighed between 350 and 400lb, the TS was no more than 290lb. It had old-style petroil lubrication, kickstarting and drum brakes (albeit the front one was a potent-looking 21s device). Its UK price (in 1976) of £600 was 10 per cent up on that for Kawasaki's three-cylinder, disc-braked KH.

Light and fast, the 250TS provided competition for the Japanese two-strokes.

The electronically sparked engine, on 25mm Dellortos, produced 30bhp at 7,000 revs, though worthwhile power was restricted to the 5,000–7,000rpm zone. High-rev getaways could be impressively fast, for the capacity, a slick gearbox with well-chosen ratios contributing to sub-16 second quarter-mile times.

Specification

250 TS (1976) *Twin-cylinder, two-stroke. 231cc (56 x 47mm). Five-speed gearbox. Tyres, 3.00 x 18in (fr), 3.25 x 18in (r). 90mph.*

Moto Guzzi Le Mans

The 750 Sport was good; the Le Mans was better. Much better. It was imported into the UK in 1976. In the transformation from 750 to 844cc, the stroke was stretched by 8mm and the compression ratio raised from 9.8 to 10.2:1; the square-type carburettors were replaced by 36mm Dellortos with velocity stacks.

There were other changes, of varying importance. Overall gearing was lowered, despite a power increase to 80bhp at 7,300rpm, boosting acceleration and general response; the clip-ons

were set a trifle higher; and the throttle action was improved, with a fulcrum device fitted at the carburettors in place of the individual cable linkage of the earlier machine.

Cosmetically, the differences were striking. More than one observer had remarked, earlier in the life of the vee-twin Guzzi, that the engine was not a thing of beauty. "Brutish" was a popular adjective for it. In Le Mans form the engine remained brutish but for the first time it was integrated into a package where it contributed as much to the bike's good looks as the frame, tank and wheels.

The chassis had an inspired colour finish. Tank, mudguards, side panels and new headlamp cowl (with "flyscreen") were in Italian racing red. With this striking colour went artfully deployed areas of matt black, a theme picked up by the exhaust system and long, slender – and none-too-comfortable – seat.

Top speed of the Le Mans was almost 130mph. Stopping power was equally impressive, thanks to three 11.5in-diameter disc brakes operating through coupled controls. The finish, in general, was not so impressive, especially on the exhaust pipes where matt-black was

Engine of the V7 – "not a thing of beauty".

The 750 Sport was long, low and fast.

133

By 1975 the Sport's side panels read 750S and front-wheel braking was entrusted to twin discs.

usually revised within weeks to matt-red, as rust appeared and spread. Le Mans owners, in the main, were undismayed. They may have considered rust some sort of tribute to hard, fast riding. One rider wrote: "Pounding up the A1 under 90-degree sunshine I could almost fantasize that the road signs read Cannes instead of Doncaster. That's what the Le Mans is all about, pure hedonistic escapism."

Specification

Le Mans (1976) *Vee-twin, ohv, four-stroke. 844cc (83 x 78mm). Five-speed gearbox. 5g fuel. Tyres, 3.50 x 18in (fr), 4.00 x 18in (r). 130mph.*

Moto Guzzi Le Mans II

By 1980 the Le Mans had been developed to MkII pitch. Basic differences were few; what changes had been made were mainly of an ergonomic and cosmetic nature. The miniature cowling round the headlamp had gone. In its place was a three-piece fairing complete with a console allowing a tidier

grouping of an extended range of instruments, together with some rearrangement of controls.

The round headlamp of the MkI had been replaced by an oblong unit (with, as before, 45/50 watt lighting) held in a shapely nose cone incorporating a dashboard and direction indicators. Matching Veglia speedometer (on the left) and rev-counter dials were larger and flanked by clock and voltmeter; below these was an array of warning lights for generator, oil pressure, brake fluid, high beam, neutral and indicators.

As fascinating as ever, and even more handsome, in MkII form, this sporting Guzzi remained obdurately third-rate in its finish-quality. In the most comprehensive road-test report yet published Val Ward had this to say: "Though major components look set for years of faithful service, the finish varies from average to pathetic, and vanishes at the double below the machine's waistline. Corrosion soon takes hold. With any bike, let alone one costing £2,600, finish like this verges on the unacceptable. It was during a visit to the enamellers that I realised how infuriating

Ted Davis of Letchworth and early Le Mans. His words: "Standing still, it looks as if it's doing 100mph!"

Controls of the 1976 Le Mans.

Guzzi finish can be. The owner of a MkII (garaged every night, enthusiast-maintained, etc) was delivering the rusty bones of his machine for complete respray after only 11,800 miles."

By the time Ward's test was concluded, his Guzzi was suffering from corrosion on sundry nuts and bolts, rear balance pipe and clamps. There were other faults, too: fluid leaked from an hydraulic reservoir ... the quartz clock lost half a minute a week ... the indicator switch was like a hair trigger ... the front of the seat had rubbed off some tank lining ... dirt had been caught in paint on the inner faces of both side panels ... a fork leg oil seal leaked.

How did Ward conclude his test report? With a curse? A vow never to press another Guzzi starter button? Hardly. Moto Guzzi charisma – the word has to be used – conquers all. "I'll take the Guzzi. It is the most satisfying modern large-capacity machine of my experience."

Specification

Le Mans II (1980) *Vee-twin, ohv, four-stroke, 844cc (83 x 78mm). Five-speed gearbox. 5g fuel. Tyres, 3.50 x 18in (fr), 4.10 x 18in (r). 137mph*

Improved control layout of the Le Mans II.

Crisp lines of the third-series Le Mans.

Moto Guzzi Spada

In 1978 Moto Guzzi augmented their vee-twin range with the Spada – "sword" – and moved into direct competition with BMW. The German makers, with the faired RS model, appeared to have captured the "fast-tourist" market. The Le Mans was too sporting, in looks and performance, to be considered as an alternative, and the other Guzzi models were ruled out because of precisely opposite reasons. The Spada took on the RS fair and square. Like the flat-twin it had a factory-tested fairing and screen and, like the second-series BMW, current in 1978, was equipped with cast-alloy wheels and disc brakes front and rear.

A not unimportant difference was that its price, at £2,300, was £700 less.

With much the same engine as that fitted in the auto V1000, the Spada had a top speed of 112–115mph, high enough to put it into contention with the RS, which was usually credited with 120mph.

Instrumentation was second-generation CEV. Signor de Tomaso had no intention of following the example of some fellow manufacturers – most notably Laverda – who had despaired of the Italian industry, and placed orders with Japanese accessory firms. Distinguished by an assortment of highly coloured switches and buttons, the new CEV equipment was comprehensive and efficient. There were speedometer and rev-counter plus a Veglia quartz clock and a voltmeter, together with a range of warning lights for indicators, neutral, oil level, brake fluid and headlight beams.

Falling short of German standards in finish, the Spada was also more vibratory and lumpy, and no better in the transmission department, its gear change having much of the BMW's "agricultural" quality that only study and practice on the part of a committed owner could ameliorate.

But the brakes – interconnected 12/11in Brembo discs – were better; and riding comfort, too, was generally agreed to be an improvement.

The Spada: competition for the BMW range.

Specification

Spada (1978) *Twin-cylinder, ohv, four-stroke. 949cc (88 x 78mm). Five-speed gearbox. 5g fuel. Tyres, 4.10 x 18in. 114mph.*

MV Agusta

In 1976 MV Agusta retired from racing after amassing no fewer than 38 individual world titles, 37 manufacturer's awards and 4,000 race wins. These statistics earned MV a place in the *Guinness Book of Records* as manufacturer of the world's most successful motor cycle. Honda or Yamaha may have edged ahead in the intervening years; but probably not.

If Norton. in the UK were open to criticism for neglecting their roadsters in favour of the racers, the same may be said, but with greater justice, of MV Agusta. In the case of the Italian form,

however, accusations of this nature lose point when it is appreciated that Count Domenico Agusta ran his business on autocratic principles, with no thought of

Luigi Taveri, of Switzerland, at Ballacoar in the Isle of Man, 1957. This ranks as one of MV's "off" years, for Taveri on the 125 was the highest-placed rider for the Gallarate firm in the world championships, finishing second in class.

Carlo Ubbiali, MV Agusta, winning the 1955 125cc Italian Grand Prix from Hans Baltisberger (NSU). The 125 dohc MV was little changed from birth in 1950 up to 1960, when for the third successive year it provided Count Agusta with a class win in the world championship, to match similar sweeps in the 250, 350 and 500cc categories. In total, MV took no fewer than four 125 world titles, three with Ubbiali as rider.

satisfying market needs with a programme of worthy production motor cycles. He was rich. He wanted to build the best – the most successful – racing motor cycle. If there was money to be made from selling ordinary motor cycles to the public, well and good, he would do so; but only on his terms, and as an adjunct, no more, to the race programme. Thus racing MVs were always interesting, and at their best remarkable, while roadsters bearing the name tended to be overpriced, overweight and underpowered.

His father's aviation business passed to Domenico in 1927 and he built it up through world-wide sales. Motor cycles, postwar, appeared to offer scope for his ambitions to excel in a field that was not dominated by state-controlled corporations, as was the case in aeronautics.

The story of the racing MVs is well documented. In these pages it may suffice to outline some of the more important stages in their quarter-century development.

After an inauspicious beginning, with two-strokes, Agusta realised that he had to turn to the four-stroke. He hired the best talent. On 1 January 1950 Pietro Remor left Gilera and joined MV Agusta at Gallarate. Remor it was who planned the transverse four racer that became the Gilera Rondine, and after the war masterminded the air-cooled version. It did not take long to complete a similar machine for his new employer.

As Remor joined MV, so details of a new dohc 125 single, already on the stocks, were released to the press. Not unlike a scaled-down version of a 250 Benelli, the single had its camshaft driven by a rightside train of gears, which also drove the magneto, mounted at the front of the crankcase. Hairpin valve springs were exposed. Lubrication followed the dry-sump principle. A

First outing on a 125 for Provini, at Modena in 1958, following his move from Mondial.

In 1954-55 the 125 was bored out to 203cc. The new single proved fast and reliable enough to win the IoM 250 TT, with Bill Lomas as rider. Twin ohc contributed to peak rpm of 10,400. The gearbox is a five-speeder. The front hub carries twin brakes.

Examples of the 203 later found their way to England where they were ridden by Minter and Hailwood, among others.

single-camshaft model was built for sale to private entrants. Although changes were made in later years, the twin-cam design was the basis of all subsequent MV racing singles. It was good enough to contribute six individual, seven manufacturer's world titles and seven IoM TT wins to MV's 1976 record.

The 500 was, of course, very like the Gilera four. The main external difference was in the disposition of the spark plugs, which inclined outward instead of being central, and upright, in Gilera fashion. Both Gilera and MV had duplex cradle frames and pivoted-fork rear suspension with springing by torsion bars and friction dampers. But the MV differed in having parallel arms, each side, for the rear fork, with the link joining the two at the rear carrying the wheel spindle. Torsion bars were also used for the front

girder fork. Total weight was said to be 290lb, with 50bhp available at 9,500rpm. Top speed was in the region of 130mph, depending on gearing.

Leslie Graham, who joined MV from AJS in the last months of 1950, was responsible for significant changes. Telescopic front forks were fitted, and conventional spring units at the rear. In 1952 the engine came in for treatment. The cylinders, with new bore/stroke of 53 x 56.4mm (later 52 x 58mm), were cast separately, instead of being formed as a single block. Power output rose to 60bhp at 10,500rpm. The rear fork lost its parallelogram form. Earles-type forks replaced the teles. Handling improved.

In 1954 the all-conquering 125, ridden by Ubbiali, was joined by a bored-out version, the twin-camshaft 203. A full 250, comprising in effect a pair of 125s

John Surtees on the 1959 four.

mounted side by side on a common crankcase, was tried at Monza, finishing fourth.

A more detailed description of this fascinating racer is given later in this section.

In 1958, after an otherwise general withdrawal from racing by the major Italian firms, MV were left as the dominant force in international grands prix, and celebrated by taking all four solo titles, from 125 to 500cc. They did the same in 1959, and in 1960.

Another succcessful race design, first employed by MV in 1964, was the 350 three-cylinder. It followed the layout and general construction of the fours, with cylinders inclined and set transversely in the frame. There were four valves to each head, dohc, and a seven-speed gearbox.

By 1975 MV had enjoyed a tremendous run of victories over a period of 17 years. Every battle had been won. There seemed to be little

point in carrying on. The three had been short-lived, the fours were ageing, the Japanese were clearly going to sweep all before them. Giacomo Agostini obliged MV with a final scintillating win in a classic meeting at the Nurburgring in 1976. World-championship racing had brought many laurels but had cost MV dear. It was rumoured that family estates had been sold to finance the last years of racing. The roadsters on sale to the public had not contributed much to MV finances. The only memorable ones were those fashioned on the racing fours: the ugly 600 of 1967, through to the beautifully styled 1,100cc GP, reputed to produce 116bhp and available, briefly, in West Germany in the late 70s.

MV Agusta 500 Racer

Some twenty years ago Mike Hailwood won the 1963 Senior TT in the Isle of Man at the then record speed of 104.64mph.

Few changes were made to the four in the years to 1963, when this Senior TT shot of Mike Hailwood was taken.

He said: "I'm still learning how to ride the MV. I know that it is capable of higher speeds than I have managed to date." Power output of this remarkable four, almost unchanged since 1956, was thought to be over 60bhp at 10,000rpm. Hailwood was timed on the Highland section of the course at a shade under 150mph. In the 1980s the big Japanese racers develop in the region of 130bhp and exceed 175mph during a TT race. The differentials reflect the pace of progress but do not diminish the standing of MV Agusta.

The four-cylinder racer, which had its first IoM win in 1956, when John Surtees rode one to lead the Senior event from start to finish, was the work of Ing. Remor, who had earlier designed the almost equally successful Gilera four. Remor came to MV at Milan in 1950. His first MV layout made use of shaft final drive. The front forks were girders, the rear pivoted fork had hand-set friction dampers. Handling, with the racer in this form, left much to be desired. The Gileras, by contrast, seemed totally modern, giving their riders a much easier time and producing 10–25 per cent more power.

Changes were made in 1951, when Leslie Graham joined MV as chief rider. The gearbox was modified, to allow the final shaft to be replaced by chain, and the girder forks were replaced by, first, a telescopic fork and then an Earles-type layout employing hydraulically damped spring units. After Graham was killed (in a second-lap crash in the 1951 Senior TT) another Englishman, John Surtees, joined the team and initiated further modifications, including a final change-over to conventional telescopic front forks, and a much improved full duplex frame.

By 1964 the 500 MV had won several world championships, two with Hailwood as race leader. Youngish motor cyclists accustomed to Japanese fours may see the MV layout as being quite conventional; in its time, though, among its contemporaries, it was (with the Gilera) outstandingly innovative.

The design was essentially that of four

Giacomo Agostini, "favourite son" of the MV concern, on the four.

125s arranged side by side. The crankshaft was supported on six main bearings (which were reputed to last two years), with complete flywheel discs for each throw. The bearings were in the form of rollers at each end of the crankshaft, with plain units between each flywheel section. Steel connecting rods ran on caged-roller big-ends, with small-end bushes in white metal (unless, as sometimes happened, these were dispensed with to permit the gudgeon pins direct fitting in the small-end eye). Shallow hemispherical combustion chambers were machined in a one-piece cylinder head; the pistons had three compression rings and the compression ratio was approximately 11.5:1. Twin overhead camshafts were driven by gears disposed in a tunnel cast between the two inner cylinders (each cylinder was separate). The valves were operated through tappets and returned to their seats by double coil springs. The original straight-through pipes were abandoned early in favour of a megaphone-equipped system, first in the form of a double siamesed layout and finally as one pipe per cylinder.

Carburation was by Dellortos, one for each cylinder, with all intakes converging towards the centre line, presumably to avoid the rider's knees. Carburettor bore was 26mm, with one float chamber between two instruments. Fuel consumption was said to be 18–20mpg.

Primary drive by straight-cut gears was used in conjuction with a five-speed gearbox mounted in unit with the engine. The clutch had three plates. The sump held six pints of oil.

Light-alloy wheels carried 10in-diameter drum brakes, twin at the front, single at the rear, with sls operation.

Specification

MV Agusta Racer (1964) *Four-cylinder, ohc, four-stroke. 500cc (52 x 58mm; later 53 x 56mm). Five-speed gearbox. Various fuel capacities. Tyres, 3.00 x 19in (fr), 3.50 x 19in (r). 148mph.*

The original MV roadster four of 1965 was big and ugly – more duck than duckling. Its dual-carburettor, 592cc engine, visually akin to the fabled racer's, was hard pressed to give a satisfactory performance. Interestingly, a much handsomer roadster four, based on the racer, had been shown as early as 1950/51 but was not put into production.

MV Agusta 750S America

As a roadster, the MV four did not take the motor cycling world by storm. In its first showing on public roads, in Italy in 1965, it had a 600cc (58 x 56mm) engine inclined in a duplex-tube frame. The engine looked impressive (despite use of only two carburettors) but little else about the newcomer's appearance appealed to a public accustomed to the aggressive looks of the four-times champion racer. With a finish predominantly in black, slab-sided tank, high-rise handlebars, big, rectangular headlamp and touring-type mudguards, the 600 was near to being downright ugly. And, contradicting pre-launch leaks that hinted at blinding speed, the few test reports to be published had to admit of quite ordinary performance, with a true top speed closer to 100mph than 110mph.

Power output was claimed to be 50bhp, on a compression ratio of 9.3:1. Weight was more than 500lb. There were two 215mm-diameter discs for front-wheel braking and a single 200mm drum in the rear wheel.

Sales were minimal, and mainly confined to Italy, in the years from 1965 as first Hailwood and then Agostini on their fours consolidated the factory's hold on the world championships. It was 1970 before the autocratic proprietor was persuaded to abandon the ungainly 600 and launch, instead, an unashamed copy of the current racer, with a capacity boost to 750cc.

In place of black went generous areas of red (even on the humpback dualseat), and the tank was restyled and tricked out in blue and white, with good-size lettering for the maker's name. New exhaust arrangements included four megaphone-style silencers, in place of the original barrel-shaped pair. Each cylinder had a carburettor. The forks were polished and – a curious but effective change – the front discs were dropped in favour of a 10in-diameter, full-width hub to accommodate twin drum brakes. Usually garbed in a factory-styled fairing, the new 743cc (65 x 58mm) four had all the good looks in the world . . . and, with 69bhp on tap, a sufficiency at least in power to back up the good looks.

The 750 was sold in small numbers in the UK. Though it was much admired high pricing prohibited more than peripheral sales, to a well-heeled minority. A later variation was the 788cc (67 x 56mm) America, which was claimed to put out 85bhp at 8,500rpm and was intended to appeal to free-spending Americans. It didn't, appar-

As concessioned by Gus Kuhn of south London, the 750 four was available in two styles, the GT being the tourer – but definitely *grand* touring – version.

In later, handsome 750S form, with twin-disc front brake and drum rear.

MV four known, briefly, as the Boxer.

ently. In a concluding phase, from 1977 to 1979, the four was stretched first to 832cc (69 x 56mm), then to 862cc (70 x 56mm) and finally to 955cc (70 x 62mm), during which time it was known by a succession of model names, such as Boxer (a title which didn't make much sense, because the engine was a straight four – and, anyway, Ferrari noticed and objected on "copyright" grounds), Monza, Arturo Magni and Ago. The 955 had 30mm Dellortos, ran on a cr of 10:1 and was said to produce almost 100bhp.

Nottingham-based Val Ward has written the most informed appraisal of the fours that has yet appeared. His first-hand experience was with a 788 Sport America, and the final paragraph of his report is significant.

"Invading the world of motorcycling's jet set was a very pleasant experience," he wrote, "but financially punishing. I wanted to ride it all the time . . . but a journalist can't keep it in petrol."

Earlier he had commented on the exhaust bellow, the "whining and clicking" from the valve arrangements, the idiosyncratic – but in the final analysis impressive – handling, the temperamental engine behaviour in extended traffic work, the "sure and powerful" brakes (in 1979 back to twin discs plus drum).

Yours – in the 1970s – for the price of any two commonplace 750s from other manufacturers.

The truth is that ordinary standards of judgment are best suspended, or forgotten altogether, for the MV never was intended for everyday use. Ideally suited to a friendly climate and wealthy ownership, the MV four was, and is, a plaything for a sunny hour. Strange, then, that Ward's researches turned up evidence of perhaps 150 of these perishable thoroughbreds stashed away in damp, impoverished Britain.

Specification

750S America (1979) *Four-cylinder, dohc, four-stroke. 788cc (67 x 56mm). Five-speed gearbox. 5.25g fuel. Tyres, 3.50 x 18in (fr), 4.00 x 18in (r). 130mph.*

MV Agusta 350 Sport

A cynical commentator said of Walter Mondale (who?), in the runup to the 1984

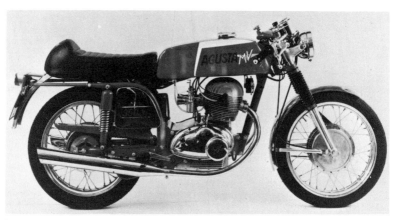

In 1973 this 350 was introduced to the UK.

Advertised as a "scrambler", complete with headlamp and horn, the heavyweight 350 was not a success.

The 1975 350S. Vibratory, speedy and expensive, it appealed to few in the UK.

US presidential election, "Why vote for an imitation when you can get the real thing!" (Mr Reagan being the real thing.) Much the same was said, in interested circles in 1977–78, of MV's 350 Sport when it was compared, to its considerable detriment, with the real – and less expensive – thing available from Moto Morini.

The 350 was one of Count Agusta's less convincing gestures to appease a road-riding public raised on the legend of MV invincibility on the race track. It *looked* fine, of course, with much racing red in view on a close-fitting fairing, a superbly designed and crafted frame, and alloy-spoke wheels bearing cast-iron disc brakes. Where it disappointed was in the power plant, hidden but not unheard behind the fibreglass, which turned out to be a 60s-designed parallel twin with pushrod-actuated valves. Reputed to put out 34bhp at 8,500rpm, this venerable unit – never, surely, a front-runner even in younger days – was rarely tested to the limit, for vibration was so intense that 65–70mph was as high as most riders were prepared to go.

Specification

350 Sport (1977) *Twin-cylinder, ohv, four-stroke. 349cc (63 x 56mm). Five-speed gearbox. 5g fuel. Tyres, 2.75 x 18in (fr), 3.25 x 18in (r). 100mph.*

Parilla

In the same way that a dozen or more new firms sprang into some kind of prominence in late-40s Britain, fresh names were added to the ranks of the established Italian manufacturers following the end of World War II. Where most newcomers in the UK relied on Mr Villiers for power, and deployed their creative energies mainly in the area of frame and suspension design, the Italians appeared to have little difficulty in evolving individualistic power units, usually of advanced ohc type.

In 1946 Giovanni Parrilla (he dropped an "r" in naming his motor cycles) designed, built and raced a single-cylinder 250. At first equipped with a single overhead camshaft, it was rejigged to take dohc and a set of exposed hairpin valve springs. Bore and stroke were 56 x 72mm and compression ratio was 7.8:1. Power was given as 21bhp and top speed as 100-plus.

Manufacturing costs must have been low in those early postwar days in Italy. That – or Signor Parrilla was moneyed from some other source; whatever the background to his advancement, the record shows that within a year he was producing a range of road machines sized at 98, 125 and 250cc and experimenting with a 250 racing twin. Designer Soncini was engaged in 1952–53 and introduced an improved roadster range which included the interesting 175cc Turismo Speciale, featuring short pushrods operating from a camshaft located at the top of the timing case.

In the 1950s the most notable Parilla was the 98cc Slughi (desert hound; Parrilla had a weakness, like English makers in a previous decade, for naming his models after dogs). Externally akin to the handsome Aermacchi Chimera, the Slughi had a spine frame of box-girder construction running from the steering head to the rear number plate. What seemed to be a shapely fuel tank was in fact the front part of an enclosed storage area; fuel was carried in a container under the seat. Encased in detachable panels, the horizontal four-stroke engine was suspended from the single frame girder in a conventional mid-wheels position and drove through a four-speed, in-unit gearbox.

The Slughi's designer, Piero Bossaglia, was engaged to plan a pair of racers for the 125 and 250cc classes. They appeared in 1959 and were, in a racing context, as straightforward as the Slughi had been unusual. Valve operation for both engines – singles – was by dohc, gear-driven in the case of the 54 x 54mm 125 and, for the 72 x 61mm 250, by shaft and bevels. Neither enjoyed great success; fifth place in the Argentine GP of 1962 was probably a high point.

Experiments in the early 60s with a 125 rotary-valve two-stroke allied to a five-speed gearbox were abandoned. Money became short. In 1967 Signor Parrilla called a halt to motor cycle production. Within a year Milan lost two of its more interesting manufacturing enterprises in the closure of Parilla and Bianchi.

Rumi

Rumi 250 Racer

Introduced in 1952, this dohc twin was quite unlike the famous Rumi scooters. It was, by Italian racer standards, of conventional layout and specification. The parallel-twin engine, forward-inclined in a massive duplex frame, drove a rear shaft through an in-unit four-speed gearbox. Rear suspension

Signor Parrilla's 250 Parilla in 1947. The sohc is driven by shaft and bevels, Norton style, with the magneto behind the cylinder.

was by pivoted fork, with movement controlled by extra-long, tipped-back telescopic units, while the front wheel was carried in a leading-link fork. The brakes were of 9in diameter, in full-width alloy hubs.

Specification

250 Racer (1952) *Twin-cylinder, dohc, four-stroke. 250cc (54 x 54mm). Four-speed gearbox. 4g fuel. Tyres, 3.00 x 18in. 110mph (est.).*

A few years on, and the 250 Parilla has gained another ohc and a forward-mounted magneto. In this pure racer form, the 250 was credited with a power output of more than 20bhp.

The most interesting scooter of the 1950s, the Rumi Formichino (Little Ant) was powered by a forward-racing 125cc two-stroke twin set at mid-wheelbase in a light, rigid body formed of aluminium pressings. Front suspension is by leading-link fork; at the rear, rubber controls movement of a single, leftside arm doubling as a casing for the rear-drive chain.

Vespa

Vespa GL2

Some analysis of the 125 Vespa, as produced under licence from Piaggio by Douglas at Bristol, may serve to make clear why this runabout, once scorned, had by the mid-1950s virtually killed off the traditional ride-to-work lightweight motor cycle in Britain. The Vespa, even when made to the possibly less exacting standards of the English licensee, retained much of the quality of the Italian original. Its fluent power and rugged construction survived the years to surprise the diehards who might, in an unguarded moment, have admitted its appeal to the uninformed tastes of commuter masses, but gave it no hope of long-term durability. How wrong they were! The Vespa – and to a lesser degree, the Lambretta – proved to be better engineered and a better performer, in almost every respect, than conventional motor cycles of similar engine capacity.

In 1954 Douglas had been turning out Vespas for five years. It was decided that the original G model, largely unchanged in the interim, should be given a facelift. Rather more than a cosmetic improvement, in fact, for the alterations were of a fundamental nature. New measurements were adopted for the GL's engine. From 56.5 x 49.8mm, when the unit produced 4bhp at 4,500rpm, a "square" configuration of 54 x 54mm (123.67cc) became the basis for a lift to 5bhp at 5,000rpm, on a compression ratio of 6.5:1.

Flexibility was improved, mainly by attention to "breathing" and stiffening of the crankcase, which gained through bolts to join the halves in place of the original studs. Fully machined flywheels were installed where before rather rudimentary bob-weights had sufficed, and the mainshafts were supported on larger-diameter ball journals. Much work had been done to improve combustion. In the new layout two transfer ports took the place of the previous single passage and combined with the angled piston crown to direct incoming petroil mixture towards the sparking plug, inclined at 45° in what the designers termed, in contradictory style, the "flat, hemi-spherical" combustion chamber.

The enhanced turbulence and flame travel resulting were teamed with the extractor effect of an enlarged and unobstructed exhaust port, positioned on the underside of the cylinder. Where the finning on the light-alloy head was previously horizontal, the new pattern was vertical, presenting a larger area to cooling air from the forced-draught fan. A new design of silencer was claimed to assist in reducing carboning-up, scourge of a petroil-lubricated two-stroke in the 1950s. It consisted primarily of a largish, oblong expansion box lined with glass wool and housing a blanked-off tube with carefully formulated apertures.

The transmission, now dealing with an extra horsepower, was suitably strengthened; an additional plate was inserted in the clutch and there was some enlargement of gearbox shafts and bearings. Gear whine, announced Douglas, had been eliminated by substitution in the drive train of a tongue-and-groove joint for the original sliding helical gear. Few scooterists would have detected the improvement; they were, in the main, of an unmechanical bent and, being devoted to personal survival, tended at all times to wear snug-fitting helmets, which muffled the sound of minor imperfections.

Thrust faces throughout the gears were enlarged, additional bearings introduced, and the kickstarter components strengthened. Gear ratios were raised a trifle, to 4.85 (which was quite high), 7.6 and 12.2 to 1. An oil seal on the main transmission shaft, once of steel-shell construction, was disgarded in favour of a rubber pattern, with the aim of curing a tendency for lubricant to seep into the rear brake drum (which itself was modified in the interests of water and grit exclusion).

Suspension improvements included attention to the hydraulically damped rear unit, and use of a stronger trunnion block on the front trailing link.

Years after the time of the GL2, Vespas were little changed from the early models. This is a 1978 150.

The detailed nature of the modifications carried out to what was, after all, a modest, cheaply priced runabout, was a pointer to the serious approach of Piaggio – and, following the Italian firm, its partners overseas – to the business of getting the world on to two tiny wheels.

Specification

GL2 (1954–55) *Single-cylinder, two-stroke. 124cc (54 x 54mm). Three-speed gearbox. 1.1g fuel. Tyres, 3.50 x 8in. 42mph.*

Index